WHAT'S SO BAD ABOUT GUILT?

Learning to Live With It Since We Can't Live Without It

Harlan J. Wechsler, Ph.D.

Simon and Schuster
New York   London   Toronto   Sydney   Tokyo

Simon and Schuster
Simon & Schuster Building
Rockefeller Center
1230 Avenue of the Americas
New York, New York 10020

10   9   8   7   6   5   4   3   2   1

Library of Congress Cataloging in Publication Data
Wechsler, Harlan J. (Harlan Jay)
   What's so bad about guilt?: learning to live with it since we can't
live without it/Harlan J. Wechsler.
      p.   cm.
   Includes bibliographical references (p.   ).
   1. Guilt.   2. Guilt—Religious aspects—Judaism.   3. Pastoral
counseling (Judaism)   I. Title.
BJ1471.5.W43   1990
296.3'2—dc20   89-28568
                                                       CIP

ISBN 0-671-67391-2

To Gerson D. Cohen

Acknowledgments

Many people have had a hand in bringing this book to life, and I am so grateful to them all. To

Carla Glasser, who suggested to me that a long-term interest I had in the subject of repentance had another side, an even more interesting side, which was guilt, and who not only planted the idea, but watered and cared for it from the time it began to sprout until it became a fully developed, many-branched tree.

Marc Jaffe, who worked with me on an early version of some of these chapters and who encouraged me to go further and to turn those chapters into a book that would see the light of day.

Arlene Modica Matthews, who read and edited every chapter soon after it came out of the printer, and whose many suggestions have made an enormous contribution to every page.

Robert Asahina, who belived in this book, who encouraged me to write the kind of book that was right for me, and who truly made it possible.

Laura Yorke, who went over the text with a fine-tooth comb and who made it so much better as a result.

Neal Kozodoy, who, as friend and supporter, has guided me and has shared with me the ways of a writer.

My rabbinical colleagues, students, and congregants, who have heard me teach much of the material in this book and who have helped me both to understand it better and to apply the vast history of ideas to the real events of living.

My teachers, whose ideas are woven throughout this book, and especially two of them who have passed on to eternal life: Paul Ramsey, Christian moral theologian, who introduced me to the rich history of Christian moral thought, and Seymour Siegel, Jewish moral thinker, who guided me through the rich world of Jewish moral thought.

The libraries and their staffs of The Jewish Theological Seminary of America, Union Theological Seminary, The Southwest Harbor Public Library, The New York Public Library, and The Society Library.

Others like Belinda Loh and Jean Griffin, each of whom played an important part. And I feel guilty, even now, for all those I have not mentioned specifically and whose help and encouragement have meant so much. Please forgive me.

My wife, Naomi Friedland-Wechsler, and my children, Ezra Micah and Hannah Leah Friedland-Wechsler, who lived with this book for years. They rode the roller coaster of its life, lived with it on vacations and throughout the rest of the year and were a great source of encouragement.

This book is dedicated to a great scholar and leader, Dr. Gerson D. Cohen, Chancellor Emeritus of the Jewish Theological Seminary of America. It was Dr. Cohen who, many years ago, offered me the opportunity to study "Jewish Moral Theology." He encouraged me and facilitated my study with Professor Ramsey at Princeton. An extraordinarily good critic for my earliest efforts at theological writing, his vast learning and unusual vision helped to steer my life on a special course, a course that made it possible for me to be a pulpit rabbi who has always had a foot in the academic world. It is the creative tension between what I have seen in my service to congregants and what I have discovered in books and in the discipline of academics that has ultimately made it possible for me to write *What's So Bad About Guilt?*

Tam v'nishlam, shevah l'el boreh olam.

Finished and complete—Praise to God, Creator of the universe!

August 1989

Contents

PART I
Defining Guilt

CHAPTER 1
What Is Guilt?

What is our innocence,
what is our guilt?
All are
naked, none is safe.
—**Marianne Moore, "What Are Years?"**

Lately I've been feeling guilty about my
guilt feelings.
—**Ziggy, the cartoon character**

Guilt is all around. It seems to blow in with the wind like crab grass, and is about as difficult to banish from a person's life. For many people, guilt *is* life.

I remember the father of a bride. He, his wife, and his daughter were all so nervous the day of the wedding, they could have lit the city's lights. Instead, they joked with one another before the ceremony, easing the tension they felt. The two women reminded him of his many faults, and he, for his part, pleaded with them to stop. "I am already guilty enough," he said with a laugh. "Guilt is the story of my life."

Of his life, and of how many others?

For months now, I have been writing this book about guilt. Often I have told others about the subject of my work. The reaction is nearly always the same: "Guilt? *I* should be writing that book!"

Guilt knows no bounds. Not only is it everywhere, it is used for everything, a universal currency traded day in and day out, all over the globe.

Some people use guilt with style, flair, and brilliance. A "perfect" hostess was serving hors d'oeuvres one evening, canapés that she had diligently and lovingly prepared herself. When she came up to each of her guests, however, she offered the delicious morsels with a reminder that she had spent six hours making them taste so good. Now these canapés might have been gobbled up on their merits, but our hostess decided to pepper them with guilt. Be sure, not one remained.

I had a teacher who was a master at using guilt. When it was time for us to recite our lessons, he would call on us by saying, "Mr. So-and-so, you *are* prepared." That was followed by a long pause, and then the words, "Aren't you?" He was as skilled as a surgeon with a scalpel. His scalpel was guilt, and it cut right through our skins.

What's so bad about guilt? An awful lot.

This is a book about guilt and an analysis of a burden that each of us bears—for a burden is what guilt is. It can be manipulative and exploitive, more bitter than the worst pill. It can eat away at us, disturbing our mental well-being just the way a degenerative disease attacks and destroys our physical well-being. It is hard therefore to wave a banner and to lead a battle for the greater good of guilt!

But I am fascinated by guilt for other reasons, reasons that go beyond its pain. What intrigues me most, what surprises me, is another dimension of guilt: the hopes, the ideals, the strivings which this complex emotion stirs. After all, what's so bad about guilt? It is far from *all* bad.

I have seen guilt draw people together. A mother and her daughter, for example. The mother was, frankly, hard to take, and she had been that way all her life. She grew old and now was sick and hardly able to care for herself. The daughter, who had spent years keeping as far away from her mother as she could, was drawn back in her difficult parent's time of need.

Ambivalent though she was, this daughter knew that primitive feelings, among them, guilt, played a key role in her actions. "Was it hard on you?" I asked. "I hate to admit it," she answered. "It was hard, but really very good."

I have seen children develop a keen sense of conscience in response to guilt. I have seen husbands who have strayed rediscover their responsibilities—and sometimes even their love —toward their wives, all because of guilt. And I have been moved by people on their deathbeds, people who put their lives in order in response to their feelings of guilt.

Everywhere there are people who strive to become good human beings helped by the signals they get from a guilty conscience that also hurts.

DEFINING GUILT

Guilt is so pervasive that it may seem impossible to contemplate. That is the reaction I often receive from people when I ask them to think about guilt. "Think about guilt?" they say. "Why, it is *unthinkable!*"

But, as with so many pervasive and somewhat unpleasant facts of life, it helps to examine guilt—a factor that motivates so much behavior and that causes so much difficulty. Unless we engage in such examination we will not know whether to run away from it or toward it, whether to laugh at it or to cry as a result of it, whether to be destroyed by it or be built up from it.

Speaking about guilt is so difficult. What, after all, is guilt?

Is guilt a feeling, or a function of the intellect? Freud, who had so much to say about guilt, actually used two German words to talk about it: *Schuldgefühl* (guilt feeling) and *Schuldbewusstsein* (consciousness of guilt). His translator generally rendered both as "a sense of guilt."[1] The words, however, say a great deal, for don't we usually speak of "feeling" guilty—the visceral side of guilt? On the other hand, our minds are the places in which normally we are plagued by guilty thoughts— the intellectual side of guilt.

Is guilt a neurotic phenomenon, or is it as natural as anger, hate, fear, and love? Is guilt something you feel, which should then pass, or is it something so basic to your existence that it should be worn like a pair of contact lenses, hardly noticeable but crucial to every move you make?

As the rabbi said when he heard the good arguments put forward by both sides of the case: "You're right. And you're right, too!" Guilt is all of the above. That is what makes it so fascinating, and that is why we have turned it over to study in detail: to distinguish between the neurotic and the normal, between the plague and the prod—both of which guilt can be. These are distinctions we need to make carefully.

GOOD GUILT AND BAD GUILT

There are two sides to guilt, one good and one bad. On the one hand, guilt mirrors the mistakes that people make. When you feel guilty and it hurts, guilt is often precisely the right way to feel. On the other hand, many times when you feel guilty that is precisely the wrong way to feel. People often look into mirrors and see dirt on their faces even though there is no dirt there at all.

And even if it is right to feel guilty, that doesn't mean that guilt is not a problem. Like kitchen grease, it collects. And collects and collects.

Masses of people are burdened by guilts that should be shed for the same reason that an armadillo sheds its skin: to make room for new growth. Yet guilt feelings are so tenacious and burdensome that they may stifle growth. Like a suit of armor, they hold a person in and weigh him down.

Even worse, there are many people who *always* feel guilty. When they get up in the morning, they feel guilty. They remember all the things they did not do yesterday that they should have done. They remember their real or imagined misdeeds toward their parents and their children, almost all at once, in a sensation that is unpleasant and powerful, especially on an empty stomach. Or they may forget the details and just feel the guilt.

Guilt is like a black fly looking for a place to bite. There seems to be no way to avoid it. Even feeling good won't help. Witness the chairman of a major television network who couldn't get too excited about his outstanding success. "I've always felt a little guilty," he said, "that I'm not only making a living, but having a good time."[2] Guilt bites like that.

Worse yet, feeling good often proves to be an invitation to guilt, such as when you suspect that happiness is really a calm before the storm, or that punishment for sins committed sometime in the past lurks like a crevasse in a glacier ready to menace the climber who is rising to the peaks.

Not long ago, a major pharmaceutical company found that someone had tampered with a few of its capsules, filling them with deadly cyanide. The chairman of the division involved then appeared on national TV, confiding that he had a premonition of trouble to come. He had just written a letter to his boss reporting a record year. He was so proud of his accomplishments. "I knew," he said, "that it was too good. Something had to go wrong." It is hard to smell the roses when it is so easy to be stung.

This is a book, therefore, about *good* guilt and about *bad* guilt too. For we live in times when the distinction between the two is commonly blurred in people's minds. It is important to know when guilt is a help and when it is a hindrance. For it can be both. We need to remember guilt's duality in order to engage it head-on. Otherwise, guilt is just an incomprehensible enemy, always lying in wait to attack.

But you can't just turn your guns on guilt. Contrary to popular opinion, it may be good to feel guilty some of the time. To control your own life, you need to be free from *unnecessary* guilt. And once you feel in control, you can go on to meet the most important challenge of all—the challenge to love.

It is hard to love when you are plagued by self-defeating, destructive guilt. Love requires an inner transformation that frees us from the burdens of our past wrongs, a goal achieved only with difficulty and aided immeasurably by all that we can learn from our *healthy, constructive* feelings of guilt.

A LADDER REACHES TO HEAVEN

When the Bible describes a night in the life of Jacob that was filled with heavenly visions, it begins by telling us that Jacob rested his head on a pillow of stones (Genesis 28:11). He had left his family the day before, and he was carrying with him enormous—and justifiable—reasons for guilt. He had tricked his father into giving him a blessing destined for his brother, Esau, and he was running away partly to escape his brother's revenge. On nights like that, a person's head rests on rocks. That is how comfortable he felt, and all of us feel, in many of the guilt-filled nighttimes of our lives.

But Jacob then saw heavenly visions. He saw angels going up and down a ladder (Genesis 28:12). Step by step, rung by rung. That, he realized, is the way to reach upward to heaven.

Hucksters come along every day and offer quick and easy remedies for every human ill. Such remedies are often proffered for guilt. But spiritual ascents are made on a ladder, not a high-speed express elevator—a ladder that requires climbing, rung by rung.

This, then, is a book of rungs, and we shall therefore move step by step in order to come to understand what guilt is, why it plays such a major role in our lives, and how to handle it so that we climb high toward the heavens instead of being stuck down on earth with our pillows of stone.

Rung by rung:

Why is it that there is so much confusion these days about guilt? Is ignoring and denying guilt an essential part of being a modern human being?

What is the function of *feeling* guilty? Why do we have such feelings and of what use can they possibly be to us?

What do we do about a guilty conscience? What role does conscience play in making us better human beings?

When should we feel guilty and when shouldn't we? And what if we punish ourselves? Does that absolve us of our guilt?

What do we say to the person who feels guilty to the core? To the person who feels choked by guilt and who feels that religion assumes that such asphyxiation is a necessary part of being a God-fearing human being? Is this what God wants from us?

How do we live with the message guilt delivers: that we are not now and never will be perfect human beings?

How do we achieve the inner liberation that comes from the

perfection of conscience and the refined awareness that make it possible to channel guilt for a greater good?

In short, then, how do we live with guilt, and how do we use it as a tool to lift ourselves up higher and higher?

The answers to these questions may have seemed obvious once, but they are not so obvious today. Therefore we shall set out on a rather unusual guilt trip: a trip designed neither to hinder nor to make life bitter, but a trip designed to bring us greater understanding about one of the most profound and ever present realities with which we live.

First, we shall define guilt. Then we shall take a look at some of the most common ways that we try to get rid of guilt, even though these methods do not work. We shall move on to see how guilt can debilitate us, and to see how we can fight back, nonetheless. We shall discover that the best way to rid ourselves of guilt is to channel it into constructive paths.

After having understood how guilt works in our own lives, we shall look beyond ourselves to the ways that guilt can transform society.

And finally, we shall see that all this analysis leads very, very high. Starting with guilt, and regardless of whether one begins with the convictions normally associated with religious faith, we shall see how this trip ends, most properly in the heavens: with the search for human purity and for the joyful feelings of love that are the ultimate purpose of religion and of guilt.

Every one of us has moments when, like that father of the bride, we say to ourselves, "Guilt is the story of my life." Every one of us learns how to use guilt like that hostess who served it up with her canapés, so that guilt becomes a tool that we wield day in and day out, a pen that writes one of the signatures by which we come to be recognized.

While we know how to feel guilty, and while we know how to make other people feel guilty, too, we do not know very well how to think about such feelings. So complex a phenomenon throws down more than the average number of roadblocks on a searching person's path.

CHAPTER 2
Our Changing Perspectives on Guilt

The emotion of guilt has been given a bum rap.
—*U.S. News and World Report*,
April 30, 1984

It was the best of Januaries and the worst of Januaries. Best because the midday sun felt like late March, the evening air gave hints of April, the snowdrops popped up even earlier than usual. Worst because of the worry that this was the greenhouse effect, already starting to warm things up.
—*The New York Times*, February 4, 1989

All the pleasure. None of the guilt.
—Advertisement for
"TCBY®" Frozen yogurt

There seems to have been a time not long ago when guilt reigned over a vast kingdom, when all her thoughtful and well-abiding citizens paid her tribute and respect. Whether that time ever really was, or whether, like a Norman Rockwell painting, it is more nostalgia than fact, the time remains deeply etched in the imagination of many of us.

It was a time when preachers *really* preached, when they turned to the Scriptures as the word of the living God and they used their voices and their bodies to shout that word to the awestruck worshipers. It was a time when the clergy had not yet studied pastoral psychiatry.

I had a teacher who, though closer to the rabbis of Lithuania than to the preachers of New England, shared the Puritans' no-nonsense approach to morality. He taught us one day what to do should a married woman come to seek counsel after having an affair. When she comes to confess her adultery, he said, do not say to her, "How interesting that is." Do not ask her about her family history or her feelings. Rather, he suggested, keep a stick in the closet and take it out on occasions like these.

Now those were the days! It was a time of fear and trembling. The golden age of guilt.

That age now seems very far away.

THE DECLINE AND FALL OF GUILT

Only a hundred years ago, Mark Twain could write, "Man is the only animal that blushes. Or needs to." Yet were a parent, teacher, or even a preacher to make such a statement today, the culprit might well be accused of "laying on a guilt trip."

I was reminded of our liberation (and of my old-fashioned teacher) when I read Dr. Laurel Richardson's study *The New Other Woman*. One of Dr. Richardson's major findings is that an affair with a married man is no longer deemed to be so terrible. More than 40 percent of married men report having affairs, and, for those with incomes over $70,000 the figure is 70 percent!

She reports, as well, that the women involved in such affairs did not regard affairs with another woman's husband as "a sin, a grievance or a breach of sisterhood." They tended to think of the marriage as temporary, considering the divorce rate, and of the wife as nonexistent. "If his wife does not exist, she cannot have feelings," Dr. Richardson writes. "If she does not have feelings, she cannot be hurt; and if she cannot be hurt, there is no reason to feel guilty."[1]

Could it be that such women are truly free from guilt, or has freedom become a rationalization for the opportunity to carry on one's life unimpeded by conventions and by other people's concerns? And what about the married men? Although Dr. Richardson does not focus on them, have they unencumbered themselves of their wives' concerns and of their marital obligations to the extent that they, too, are liberated from guilt?

Ah, for that stick!

Look what has become of guilt. We live in an age when guilt is not only mocked, it is trivialized. More people use the terms "sin" and "guilt" in relation to food, I suspect, than in relation to anything else. What is sin? A piece of cheesecake, of course.

A New York caterer has recently expanded her standard dinner-party menus by producing a low calorie/sodium/cholesterol menu which she calls, aptly, "Dining Without Guilt."[2] A chic ice-cream company has launched a full-color advertising campaign that makes your mouth water when you see its magnificent pink scoops of strawberry ice cream. The bold print at the top of the page speaks directly to consumers' hearts. "Enjoy the guilt," it says.

THE PSYCHOLOGICAL ATTACK

In many, many quarters, guilt has gone out of style. Purveyors of instant happiness routinely take out a contract on guilt, aiming their hit men at it. In a book entitled *Good-Bye to Guilt*, Dr. Gerald G. Jampolsky delivers a short course on the ways to rid a person of guilty feelings. Guilt, he contends, pollutes and destroys a human being. More than that, guilt is the product of the thought system of the ego, a way of thinking that separates human beings from one another and which is therefore at the root of evil. As a "self-made poison," guilt is the ego's tool for keeping us "hopelessly bound to our past."[3]

> Guilt is the emotion we invented. It is both our jailer and the jail. It keeps our mind imprisoned and enchained in

the bondage of self-condemnation and depression. It is the gravity that keeps us pinned to the ground, limited to a physical reality. It forbids us to awaken from our sleep, and in our dream-state we feel separate from God and our brothers and sisters.[4]

Dr. Jampolsky's book is a plea for love and an attack on love's principal enemies: guilt and the ego. Get rid of them both and the world, as well as each person in it, will know peace.

Could it be that easy?

The broad attack on guilt, however, is fueled by even more volatile ideas than those of Dr. Jampolsky. After all, we are products of an age that thinks in psychological terms. When we think of our rational minds, we think of our egos. When we think of the compelling impulses that drive us to get what we want when we want it, we think of the id. Psychological language, even psychological jargon, is commonly borrowed from the professional's office to be used to describe everyday events that take place in our everyday unprofessional lives. Psychological language becomes *our* language and we often use its terms in imprecise and unscientific ways. That is the case with guilt.

No doubt the psychiatrists and psychologists among us can tell us a great deal about *neurotic* and *psychotic* guilt. Certainly there are people who are unable to move forward, who are unable to get out of bed or unable to hold a job because they suffer from the complex and serious problems of guilt. But is guilt *by nature* neurotic? While guilt is often very painful, is it *by nature* evil, as Dr. Jampolsky would have us believe?

Many a modern person will listen to anything dressed in psychological language, decorated with a little "love" here and a little "peace" there. It seems, by the very style in which it is said, to be true. Who could be against love and peace? Who could come to the defense of so unpleasant a criminal as guilt?

There is a great deal of dangerous fallout from such ideas. For example, many of us believe that he who is guilty must be neurotic, or at least weak and impotent, for sure. Humorist and social commentator Jean Shepherd writes of a strange and undesirable form of modern man called *wimpus apologeticus americanus*—better known to the rest of us as a wimp. "He feels guilty when a plague of locusts descends on an obscure country 12,000 miles away. His first question is, 'How have I failed them? Where did I go wrong?' He is consumed by guilt." [5]

But, alas, along with such misconceptions, something else is going on which has helped lead to the decline and fall of guilt. There is a "superman" in the process of being created, one who received his impetus from Nietzsche a century ago and who has, with a little help from Sigmund Freud and some of his followers, taken his potshots at the vocabulary and world view found in the Bible and held by Western civilization for so long.

To this new man, religion is an illusion, a projection of feelings and wishes. It is childlike in its simplicity and naiveté, and best abandoned by the new man who takes responsibility for himself. According to such a view God, of course, is dead, a victim of confrontation with truth and reality.

Guilt—for what? For transgressing God's will? If there is no God, then there is no will to transgress. For transgressing one's own conscience or "superego"? There must be better ways to deal with problems than to be slaves to those boring and relentless internalized "shoulds."

Such is the vogue: to use the theological ideas of the Bible—guilt chief among them—as the convenient whipping boys of every modern ill. So throw the cloak of guilt away. Peel off layer after layer. Take away the waistcoat of sin, the headdress of modesty, the pantaloons of humility. Peel them all away, though, and what do you have? Supermen dressed in the emperor's new clothes.

Don't we deserve more?

RELIGION AND THE FALL OF GUILT

When I read the Bible I often wonder to myself how people will react to the text that created the morality of a civilization. Read the story of Adam and Eve. It is a story about guilt! Read the prophets of Israel and their endless condemnations of their people for oppressing the poor or for committing idolatry. Their story is a story of guilt. The prophets threaten exile and destruction, calamities that in fact changed the course of history. Their entire approach was designed to induce deep feelings of guilt. Guilt, the tool of Isaiah, Jeremiah, and Amos—what has now become of guilt?

The words, the feelings, the presentiments of Biblical doom are today borrowed, taken from contexts that spoke to mankind's loftiest confrontation with the weaknesses of the human spirit and the precarious nature of the human condition, and, lo and behold, they are out on loan nearly exclusively to the domain of rich foods. How many times will people react to chocolate mousse with the full store of classical religious vocabulary used formerly for weighing the sins of human deeds and the guilts of human shortcomings?

If we can successfully remove the stain of guilt from the important concerns of life, then we will successfully free love and sex, kindness and anger, the family, society, government, and everything else that matters from the burden they have carried for so long. No more guilt. Free at last.

But what does that say about us?

Now, while I am really peeved by the bad treatment that religion has received in recent times, I am not so blind as to overlook the fact that religion has contributed generously to the campaign for its own demise, an effort liberally aided by others.

A wagging finger and an authoritarian leader, are they not the images associated with religion and its purveyance of guilt? Guilt implies, as we shall see, a standard that has been transgressed. But there are ways of acknowledging standards, and there are other ways of using certainty and authority to destroy the freedom and the happiness of untold numbers of persecuted souls. Pictures of the Ayatollah Khomeini, or pictures of the Inquisition—they all convey the same idea: that religion, because it believes in authority, must be authoritarian; that religious people, because they believe in God, must be gods to themselves and to others.

These assumptions are simply not true. Religious people live *in response to God*, not in place of God. God's word for us is a loud clarion call often heard in a night of darkness, heard amidst thunder and lightning. To hear it is to be humbled by it, not emboldened by its power. In fear and trembling we look at our religious commandments and find ourselves wanting. That does not make us feel good. It does not give us a club to wield against other human beings. It does not make our lives easy, either, for it is we who have to live with and deal with our guilts —guilts formed in response to the lofty aspirations we have as children of God.

But this idea of religion, widespread though I think it is, is an idea of religion about which you seldom read. The religion of violence makes better headlines. Those who distort religion and those who distort the powerful meaning of God's presence in human life are far more attractive to the media than those who see religion as an ever-present challenge to our souls. Looters and burners and killers in the name of faith *steal the thunder,* and they become news.

The induction of guilt should not be a club wielded by the religious but rather a challenge that religion issues to human perfection. You needn't believe in burning people at the stake or cutting their hands off when they err to see the positive value of having to measure yourself against the standards of lofty religious faith. But you will, no doubt, have guilt. And therefore, guilt is both a problem and a necessity for those of us who search daily to hear the thunder and to incorporate a transcendent meaning into our lives.

Taking the club to religion by attacking guilt may be enticing. But even if religion is attacked and subdued, I think you will find that guilt will come to its funeral, dressed in secular clothes. For even the most secular of the secularists are beginning to see that you cannot banish guilt. The reality is that this obsessive compulsion with ridding ourselves of guilt is not the panacea that so many have imagined it to be. How happy, after all, are we?

IF EVERYTHING IS SO GOOD, WHY DO I FEEL SO BAD?

We live in the happiest of times. Or do we live in the unhappiest of times?

In the magazine *Self,* one of our contemporary magazines that pays tribute to the new, free, and independent self that has been whittled away from the old one rotted out by guilt, an article discusses the problem of summer having become an occasion for guilt.[6] The author looks back longingly at the old days, when summer was devoted to the single pursuit of leisure, and when leisure was incompatible with guilt.

Now, however, times have changed. For while we have plenty of leisure time, the author writes, we are enjoying it less. Now we make summer resolutions, more difficult to keep even than last New Year's resolutions. We who have more time than people have probably ever had are worried about how we use that time. And what happens? Guilt.

What seemed simple in bygone days is simple no more. "To tan or not to tan, that is the question," says the author. After all, she goes on (clearly tongue in cheek but serious nonetheless), you can't expect to look smashing in your white summer linens without a good tan. On the other hand, who hasn't heard about the strong possibility that skin cancer will be induced by those delightful summer days in the sun. "Guilty if you do," she writes, "guilty if you don't."

THE MORE YOU KNOW, THE WORSE YOU FEEL

It is not because we lack intelligence that we are in such a quandary today. It is precisely because we have more facts at our fingertips that we come to live with more and more complex possibilities of guilt. Take the case of smoking.

Nowadays you know that smoking is bad for your health. And at least once a year—let us say on New Year's Eve—you may decide to quit. Yet every would-be quitter can tell you that going "cold turkey" is really for the birds; it is a very difficult thing to do. You get along for three weeks without a cigarette and then you yield to temptation and have a smoke. If you have made your resolution properly you will also be filled with guilt.

Would you want it another way? The guilt is your best chance at being able to go back on the track and to perhaps recover the commitment you had made in the optimistic flurry of a New Year's Eve. But look what modern life has given us! Before you knew that tobacco was bad for your health, you didn't have to worry about this particular guilt. Now you do.

Or consider how the jogging boom affects our pursuit of perfection, not only in physical things but in the moral sphere as well. Masses of Americans run not only to keep their bodies in shape but for the more diffuse benefit of "well-being." To many, the pursuit of physical training has come to have an important religious dimension, for it has an impact upon the mind. It is relaxing and relieves stress, all for the good.

But ask any runner who has missed his jog today whether he knows anything about guilt, and he will write a chapter of this book. No, guilt has not gone away. In the very era of liberation, at the very time when the chains of guilt are being broken and freedom is about to dawn, guilt is very much with us.

In jogging, as in so many other modern pursuits, guilt is a by-product of the way we search for happiness. That search is so often conducted with the assumption that each of us is in the driver's seat, steering our destinies toward the goal of happiness. Like the finish line of the 26-mile marathon, the goal is there for the taking if we but apply ourselves. Many come to assume that they are all-powerful over their fates, rarely paying attention to the fact that such power exists only to a limited degree. As one commentator on the running scene explains it:

> . . . emphasis on the small domain over which the lone runner can have an effect, instead of on the larger domain over which no individual has control—including the realms of heredity, culture, and chance—has the consequence of shifting responsibility for environmental change from society to the individual, and of redefining "being ill" as "being guilty."[7]

The search for happiness and contentment leads, paradoxically, to more guilt! Where will it end?

In family life, too, guilt is all around. What are new parents discovering, those who put off childbearing so that a future mother could become established first in her career? New kinds of guilt!

In his book *How to Be a Guilty Parent*, Glenn Collins lists over eighty-five kinds of guilt that, I am sure, many parents feel.[8] Among them note: working mother guilt ("Hello, Mom? Is that you? I know you don't like me to phone you at work and all, but where's the Sweet 'n Low? I have to go give the firemen their Sweet 'n Low now. . . ."); sexism guilt ("We'll furnish her nursery in a nonsexist way, we'll choose a nonsexist name for her," etc. "And we'll never feel a bit guilty when we happen to *fail* doing any one of these fine things."); and even toy guilt ("What's that, Davie? You don't have what? You don't have an Astro Phaser 3000 Play Pak? Every other kid in your class has one? It's *our fault* that none of the other kids invite you to their house? My God, Davie, why didn't you tell me about this before? We'll get one immediately!")!

There is even a religion guilt ("Well, we always *intended* to go to church, you know?"). You see, things may be looking up after all.

Indeed, Collins's book is meant to poke fun at the complicated lifestyles led by many very modern fast-track people, but it is quite true—and as a rabbi I can bear witness to the fact—that these concerns are genuine concerns and they illustrate a unique experience that parents have always known and to which today's parents are not immune. Could it be that when you get into the deepest human experiences, such as bearing and rearing a child, you rediscover guilt?

No, guilt has not gone away. As a matter of fact, it is so much in the air that a computer software creator has been working on a computer game where you can punch in "Mom" and get a Jewish mother who appears sitting in an overstuffed chair knitting, "making you feel guilty and dispensing advice."[9] Will the software sell? If I were a betting man, I would bet on its selling very well.

Not only that: A woman has created a whole series of greeting cards with a special emphasis on guilt. They are designed to be *in loco parentis*, meaning in place of a Jewish mother. One says, for example, "Why don't you call?" I suspect that that card will do very well, too.

JEWISH GUILT

Now I am sure that it is no coincidence that the computer game and the greeting cards portray not just *any* mother, but a *Jewish* mother. While it is true that a mother doesn't have to be Jewish to wield a club of guilt, and while it is true, as well, that Jewish mothers deserve praise, not pity, for the role they play in developing the consciences of their children and for giving profound love and care to them, still the image, comic or not, does convey a certain truth. For an important thread runs throughout the Jewish tradition, one that provokes many ambivalent reactions.

Deep in the Jewish tradition, deep in the psyche of the Bible, is a human being who can experience guilt. And it is true, whether one seeks to praise the fact or to bury it very deep, that the culture of the Jews is a culture rooted in that conception of a human being. More than guilt's being a problem, it is second nature to Jews.

The comedians tell this story in a thousand ways. The latest: What is a "Jewish affair"? Answer: All of the guilt and none of the fun! Or Woody Allen's guilt trip in the movie *Manhattan*. He quits his job and ponders the financial implications. First he will have to give up tennis lessons. Then, he reflects that he will have to give his parents less money and as a result his father will not have as good a seat in the synagogue, "away from God, far from the action." The comedians pay homage to Jewish guilt!

YOU DON'T HAVE TO BE JEWISH TO BE GUILTY

But as you don't have to be Jewish to eat Levy's rye bread, you don't have to be Jewish to be an expert in guilt.

Catholics often outdo Jews in their ability to create guilt. Someone said to me recently that Catholics have original sin, while Jews have original guilt. As far as I can see, there isn't much difference between the two. And Protestants? ". . . human beings cannot accept their limitations without a sense of guilt," wrote Reinhold Niebuhr, one of the great Protestant thinkers of our century.[10] Much of Niebuhr's extraordinary writing is an effort to convince modern man that he must take responsibility for his actions and that he must judge himself by an "impossible ethical ideal" in response to which he will invariably feel guilty. Yes, even long after Martin Luther and Jonathan Edwards, Protestants still know guilt. And Moslems, too. A Moslem takes the *hajj* (pilgrimage) to Mecca and returns home guiltless as a newborn child.

What do these religions have in common? Guilt. These are the grounds on which some very fruitful interreligious dialogue could take place. We are all experts on guilt. The secular world, too, as we have seen, has not escaped.

I am amazed at the persistence of guilt. Every year, on Kol Nidre, the night of Yom Kippur, the Jewish Day of Atonement, I can't believe my eyes. That night the synagogue is filled to capacity, and the entire theme of Yom Kippur is guilt—not wallowing in it, but recognizing it and repenting in response. I look out at the congregation on Kol Nidre. Hundreds of people, as far as the eye can see. Almost as if the synagogue were a football stadium.

What is the battle? Who are the opposing teams? That battle is one against sin and transgression. The opposing teams are the many levels of the self that fight with one another and that make it so difficult to repent. And it is guilt that supplies the energy, the force that makes the battle worth fighting. "Who shall live and who shall die," the prayers say, raising the moral ante to the highest level by seeing life and death as God's response to how well we are succeeding in mastering our lives and making something of them. The response? Guilt—old-fashioned, outdated, unwanted guilt. There we are, in a house of worship filled to the rafters, and why? Because of guilt—guilt that was supposed to have withered away but has not.

This is the anomaly: the persistence of guilt. Or, to put it in a way that reflects so many of the feelings in people when they come to the synagogue on Yom Kippur, people whose lives are objectively happy and yet who are unhappy nonetheless: If things are so good, why do I feel so bad? I am plagued by guilt when I thought that at last I was free.

But why? Have we simply failed at mastering the techniques designed to rid us of guilt? Or are we forever condemned to being guilty, whether we like it or not? Is guilt part of the baggage we carry from the past, best jettisoned as soon as we know how to do so? Or do we perhaps need guilt? Is it a liability or an advantage? Perhaps both.

When you think about guilt, how do you feel? If you are like me and so many others, you find yourself on the horns of a dilemma. I described a golden age of guilt, an image from the past, which, while tantalizing in some ways is repulsive in others. Do we, who have discovered the liberating personal freedom which analysis and self-examination have given us, really want to turn back to an age of fear and trembling? Who wants to berate and beat his children? Who wants to be intimidated by parents? Who wants a world where human relations are characterized by anxiety rather than by sympathy, compassion, tolerance, and love?

Guilt? When you think about it, *you can't live with it!* But *you can't live without it* either! The pain and the glory, the agony and the ecstasy: that is the nature of guilt.

Let us look at it squarely—but not in order to achieve a new golden age of guilt. Rather, to salvage nuggets from the past that still can be used as hard currency today. For knowing how to live with guilt can help immeasurably in achieving the good life after which nearly all of us strive.

CHAPTER 3
Feeling Guilty

> *By the sympathy of your human hearts*
> *for sin ye shall scent out all the places—*
> *whether in church, bedchamber, street,*
> *field, or forest—where crime has been*
> *committed, and shall exult to behold the*
> *whole earth one stain of guilt, one*
> *mighty blood spot.*
> **—Nathaniel Hawthorne,**
> *Young Goodman Brown*

Why is it so difficult to talk seriously about guilt? Because, as we have already seen, guilt is a feeling. And it is difficult to talk about feelings.

People find it easier to talk about ideas. They divide guilt into categories and catalogue its many different varieties. The eighty-five guilts of *How to Be a Guilty Parent* are only a start. Just think where we could go from there.

But this approach is wrong. Whenever tempted to think about all the many different kinds of guilt there are, I remind myself of a cartoon that appeared in *The New Yorker*. A woman is reading the newspaper and she turns to her husband who is apparently working on the family bills. "There's so much talk these days about this kind of guilt and that kind of guilt," she says. "Isn't anybody just plain ashamed anymore?" [1]

That is precisely the question that bothers me: Isn't anybody just plain ashamed anymore? Ashamed, upset—*guilty*—these are feelings, not ideas. Guilt is more than a state of mind, though we so often treat it as a rational problem. It has an intellectual dimension, no doubt, but *feeling guilty* is what we mean, first and foremost, when we talk about guilt.

Feeling guilty—not a state of mind but an *emotional* state. There is a profound difference between the two.

Each year, as the Jewish High Holy Days of Rosh Hashanah and Yom Kippur approach, I am struck by the difference. For I am impressed once again by how easy it is to think the right thoughts, and how hard it is at the same time to change the way we act. Feelings are the key.

We rabbis commend our congregations to repent, for during these days Jews participate in a grand spiritual drama of self-renewal, a drama which is conceived, by and large, in *intellectual* terms. *Think* about what you have done wrong in the year that has just gone by, we instruct. *Think* about the kind of person you would like to be in the year that is about to come. Think, think, think! I have often asked myself: Why don't we say *feel, feel, feel?*

We are so rational and thoughtful. We are sensitive to ethics and we *think* about the ethical dilemmas we are in. All well and good. But this emphasis on the intellectual dimension of guilt reminds me of the professor of ethics at Columbia University who always liked to surprise his freshman class by attacking their preconceptions about the study of ethics. Knowing well that many students would be taking his course with the assumption that it would have a direct effect upon their lives, he would tell them, "You do not expect the professor of mathematics to be a triangle, do you? Therefore you should not expect the professor of ethics to be ethical, should you?"

That is the problem. The intellect can be sharp and comprehend the issues which make for ethical or unethical behavior. But where is the *guilty* professor? There is a gap between what the mind perceives and what the person does—because every person is a combination of intellect and emotions, and it is in the realm of the emotions that so much behavior, be it good or bad, has its source.

If we try to locate guilt, therefore, on the map of human experiences, it will help most to fix its coordinates somewhere near the human heart—the metaphorical site of the emotions.

GUILT IS AN EMOTION

In a recent philosophical study entitled *Pride, Shame and Guilt,* Gabrielle Taylor speaks of guilt as one of the "emotions of self-assessment." Though she focuses on guilt as a legal concept, she rightly places its locus in the emotions.[2] Similarly, Dr. Willard Gaylin, in a study about feelings published several years ago, includes among those feelings, guilt. Guilt, he says, encompasses feelings that range from self-disappointment and anguish to the sense of being contaminated, marked, and soiled.[3] How right he is, and how such feelings span the gulf of time.

Do you remember Michelangelo's fresco of Adam on the Sistine Chapel ceiling? What terror there is in Adam's eyes. That is the look I am waiting for from the professor of ethics!

Shakespeare captures so well the emotion of guilt. "I am afraid to think what I have done," cries Macbeth after he has killed Duncan, King of Scotland.[4] Notice that an emotion—fear—comes before the thought. Shakespeare wisely sees guilt as having its roots in a preconscious state.

The scribe Ezra long predated Shakespeare's guilt-ridden characters when he cried to the Lord on behalf of his people: "O my God, I am ashamed and blush to lift up my face to Thee, my God; for our iniquities are increased over our head, and our guiltiness is grown up unto the heavens" (Ezra 9:6).

Whether it be Isaiah, who spoke of sins being like crimson, red as dyed wool (Isaiah 1:18), Nathaniel Hawthorne, who wrote of Hester Prynne's scarlet letter, or Ezra, who pointed to a blushing face, there is a tangible, visible sense to the feelings of guilt. The red color conveys metaphorically the deep connection between such feelings and the life force that runs through our veins.

After all, what do we mean when we describe someone turning as red as a beet? Can't you feel the surge of blood, the heat, and the sweat that begins to break out?

GUILT IS A GUIDE

All that is for a purpose, though.

Guilt feelings are, first of all, an indicator, a guide. Much like pain, they function within a human being as part of the complex message system that feeds information back to us on the state of our well-being. Pain is part of the message system that indicates a problem with our physical well-being. Indeed, there are times when pain also is a manifestation of psychological illness. Guilt, however, points to problems of spiritual well-being.

Of course everyone wants to feel good. But the temptation is to take a simple pill to block out the bad feelings. If you had a serious disease, what would you do? Take an aspirin to be sure that the disease would go away? No doubt the aspirin might reduce the symptoms, but lowering the fever is surely not the same as curing the disease.

It is precisely the same for guilt. Guilt is a sign of something going on inside a human being, of something that is not right that has to be fixed up. Getting rid of the bad feelings that guilt induces may serve as a temporary treatment of symptoms. But it is not a cure. You have to look further inside for that.

Take the feelings of a man who came to see me one day. The burden of guilt he bore drew him into the synagogue.

The man's voice was filled with agony. He had embezzled a large sum of money and was to appear in court the next day to plead guilty to the charges against him. "Why then did you come to see a rabbi?" I asked. Because, he told me, even if he were to confess in court, and even if he were to pay the penalty according to the laws of the state, he would still not be able to live with himself.

"Live with yourself—why not? You will pay a penalty. You will be punished according to the law. Won't that make you feel better?" I asked. "There is something higher," he said. "Do you mean," I asked, "that there is a higher judge and that you are afraid to stand before His bar?" "Yes," he told me. "My life has been corrupted; God knows!"

The man's existence was tainted and he felt like a soiled human being. He reminded me of the psalmist who says in his despair: "My God, my God, why hast Thou forsaken me. . . . I am a worm, and no man; a reproach of men, and despised of the people" (Psalms 22:2,7).

Think about this man: he was consumed by guilt. I suspect that at some point guilt may have seemed to him like his greatest problem. Were he to have been a follower of the "feeling good" school, he would undoubtedly have thought to himself that he needed more love and less guilt so that he could feel good once again. Guilt would have been the evil. Could he abandon it, things would be good.

Yet the truth is that guilt was not the man's problem at all. Guilt was a symptom of something else. Guilt was an evident, readable barometer of this man's unsettled inner life. For this embezzler, it was an indication that, in the highest sense, he had lost respect for himself.

Or take the case of a woman, a wonderful woman, full of deep feelings, who had become a widow some while before. Now she was deeply depressed.

The woman came to tell me of her prolonged grief for the husband she loved so much. He had died several years ago, yet still she carried a burden on her heart that allowed her no relief. She could not smile with her children or with her grandchildren.

We talked for a long time. Finally the woman asked: Is it right to stop mourning for the man I loved? And I explained, in the words of Scripture, that there is a time to mourn and a time to dance, each in its own season (Koheleth 3:4). We talked more about the need to grieve fully for a person one loves and about the need, also, to end the period of grieving so that we can return to living our lives. Finally the woman looked up and smiled, renewed as she had not been for years.

This woman had been depressed, and no doubt she was plagued by guilt. Did she need some happiness pill? Guilt was a sign. To some extent she had "survivor's guilt." Like many who survive when their loved ones do not, she was plagued by the feeling that she should not be alive while her dear husband was dead. Beyond that, mourning served as a concrete way of continuing to demonstrate her deep love for him. If she stopped, it would be a way of saying that she didn't care for the man who meant everything to her.

Her guilt was a sign. It pointed to her moral fiber and it raised an issue that had to be resolved. Once resolved, she was free. If anything, guilt was the impetus that pointed her in the direction where her freedom was to be found.

The embezzler needed to recover his dignity. He had done wrong and had to pay his debts on all levels, even with God. The mourner also had to work something out. In each case guilt helped to make the problem clear.

Now it is certainly true that guilt can get out of control, that a person's indicator system can cease functioning effectively and can begin to induce its own independent problems. That happens with pain, and it can happen even more readily with guilt. The spiritual *burden* of guilt can lead to the psychological *problem* of guilt. Normal guilt can become neurotic guilt—that can certainly happen. But there is a normal guilt that functions day in and day out and that serves, through the emotions, as a window into a person's inner life.

What do we have to do then when plagued by guilt? Step number one is: Think of guilt the way you think of pain. Ask the question "How am I ill? What is the source of my pain?"

SPIRITUAL HEALTH

The method is not so unusual. As a matter of fact, the medieval Jewish philosopher Maimonides long ago compared spiritual illnesses to those that are physical.[5] And it is a *spiritual* pathology that weighs most heavily on mankind.

Expanding upon Maimonides, Rabbi Joseph B. Soloveitchik notes that "sin constitutes a sort of spiritual pathology, just as many diseases of the flesh constitute physical pathology, as when the tissues cease to behave in a normal fashion and cells begin to grow wildly—so sin is a sign of spiritual pathology."[6]

Rabbi Soloveitchik goes on to say that sin reaches human consciousness in many of the same ways that disease becomes a part of our awareness: through the language of suffering, through deep and piercing pain of the psyche, through spiritual agony.

Spiritual agony—that is what people so often feel. When someone walks through the door of my study, it is often that agony that is written into the muscles of his face. The pain is really more than psychological pain; it is *spiritual*. There is a deep unrest in a person's soul. There is a longing for a *spiritual* harmony which belies the unrest. There is a sense of searching, almost a sense that a person is climbing a mountain and is weary with fatigue. Yet the climb is an integral part of a personal quest.

We begin to talk, and often people will be ashamed to raise the matters that are on their mind. "I know this sounds stupid," they will say, "but . . ."

And then the pain begins to come out. Through a sometimes circuitous route, the story emerges. The embarrassment, however, often does not fade. "I know I should not be so upset," or "I know I should be able to control myself." Finally: "Rabbi, why do I feel so bad?"

"So that you can feel good," I say. "Your feelings have given you the strength to work out the problems of your own spirit. They have shown you where the work has to be done."

Guilt is the emotional tip-off, the prod to get us to ask: "What is the source of my discomfort?" In other words, spiritual life is very much like everyday life; say: "Ouch!" and then ask the probing question: "Where do I go from here to get rid of my pain?"

Feeling guilty is, therefore, the beginning of a process. Not the end, but the beginning. It is pain with a purpose: to guide us in a direction so that we will henceforth feel good.

CHAPTER 4
A Guilty Conscience

So full of artless jealousy is guilt,
It spills itself in fearing to be spilt.
—**William Shakespeare,** *Hamlet*

Conscience is a great servant but a
terrible master. It is somewhat like an
automobile horn. It is useful for warding
off impending danger. But if a horn gets
stuck it's a terrible nuisance.
—**Rabbi Sidney Greenberg**

Guilt, though, is not only a collection of emotional aches and pains. Combined with those pains are pangs of conscience, anxiety caused by troubling thoughts.

When James Joyce describes the anguish of his hero Stephen Daedalus, he describes this rich but troubling combination well:

He closed the door and, walking swiftly to the bed, knelt beside it and covered his face with his hands. His hands were cold and damp and his limbs ached with chill. Bodily unrest and chill and weariness beset him, routing his thoughts. Why was he kneeling there like a child saying his evening prayers? To be alone with his soul, to examine his conscience, to meet his sins face to face, to recall their times and manners and circumstances, to weep over them.[1]

The cold, the feeling of being alone, the weeping: these are manifestations of the emotional dimension of guilt. Yet there is more to guilt than that. As Joyce described it, there is the experience of meeting sins face to face, recalling the past, examining the conscience. These introduce a new and more cerebral dimension, a state of cognitive awareness. A *guilty conscience.*

Dr. Karl Menninger begins the wonderful book he wrote on sin by telling the story of a plainly dressed man who stood on a street corner of the busy Chicago Loop in September 1973, pointing at passersby and calling out to them: "Guilty!" As you can imagine, the man had a strange effect on people. One person actually turned to another and said, "How did *he* know?"

That man had no access to inside information, no psychic powers. It must have been the familiarity and universality of his charge that made him so seductive and that enabled him to get away with pointing an accusing finger without being dismissed as just another nut who hollers on street corners.

Dr. Menninger goes on: "Guilty of what? Guilty of overparking? Guilty of lying? Guilty of arrogance and hubris toward the one God? Guilty of 'borrowing,' not to say embezzling? Guilty of unfaithfulness to a faithful wife? Guilty of evil thoughts or evil plans?"[2]

Ask it any way you like, the answer to the question "Do you have a guilty conscience?" is usually simple to know. If you are alive and well, the answer is "Yes!"

I have heard it so many times. From an adulterer, filled with sorrow over deeds that never should have been done: *"I have such a guilty conscience!"* From a young wife, recently married and already troubled by stormy relations with her husband's parents: *"I have such a guilty conscience!"* From middle-aged children whose elderly, feeble parents can no longer be cared for at home and who must be placed in nursing homes: *"We have such a guilty conscience!"*

It is conscience: our mind and all of its thoughts, that is particularly stung by guilt.

A PAIN IN THE MIND

What do we mean when we say that we have a guilty conscience? Firstly, that we feel bad. But as soon as we talk about our conscience we mean something more.

While guilt is an emotion, its effect is more than emotional. Compare feeling guilty, for example, with being depressed. When you are depressed you surely feel bad. Yet you often can't put your finger on what it is that makes you feel so terrible. With guilt, you have plenty of problems, but not that particular one. With guilt, you feel bad *because.* . . . There is always some *because*, some matter that weighs heavily on your mind.

Because you didn't call . . . Your mother's birthday came and went and you forgot to call. Not only that, but it has been three weeks since you have spoken to her at all. Of course *she* could have called *you*, and perhaps she should feel guilty and maybe she even does; but you are her child, you feel the burden, you are plagued by guilt.

Because you haven't finished the job . . . Your colleague in Los Angeles needs the memo you promised over a week ago. Not that you haven't been working on ten different things, but still —he is waiting and you don't have it done.

Because you let the team down . . . Managerial guilt, *Fortune* magazine calls it. There was a meeting this afternoon and you completely forgot about it. All your subordinates were gathered in the conference room, waiting for the guidance that only you could supply. And there you sat at your desk, tied up on the telephone. You forgot to tell your secretary you had scheduled the thing, and your good, trusting colleagues didn't even feel they could call to ask where you were. You have gotten yourself overbooked and you have let the team down. You are now paid back with guilt.[3]

Because of the children . . . They need new clothes for the fall; music lessons must be arranged, supplies must be bought for school. A husband to care for, a house to care for, parents to care for, yourself to care for. Not enough time for anyone—but lots of guilt.

The manager of market research at a major company tells that his wife confronted their four-year-old daughter in anticipation of a visit from Grandma. "We're going to have a visitor," she said, "and it's someone you haven't seen in a long time. Can you guess who it is?"

"Dad?" the little girl eagerly replied.

That dad knew well a parent's guilt.

When you have a *guilty conscience* you have more than feelings; you are burdened by nagging thoughts. When you are plagued by a guilty conscience you feel it not only in your gut; you feel it in your head. When the weight of conscience presses down upon you it touches more than your nerves; it touches your imagination and your convictions. Because *a guilty conscience is a pain in the mind.*

Guilt is a feeling that poses questions: intellectual questions and moral questions. A woman may conceivably feel anger and even hatred toward her in-laws. When, as a result, she says that she has a guilty conscience, she is telling you more: that she subscribes to a view of how a person *should* relate to a parent, in-laws included, and that such a view does not square with the feelings she now has.

She may not have studied Scripture, but "Honor thy father and thy mother" rings loud and clear anyway—either because she has been taught that this is the way she *should* feel or because it is simply self-evident that parents deserve a special level of treatment. *Her thoughts tell her she should be feeling differently.* And, as a result, she has a guilty conscience.

Guilt is a feeling that hauls a person into court and places him before a judge, the conscience, who speaks out for right and wrong. A judge who never tires of reminding us that there is a tremendous gap between what we are and what we ought to be. A special judge who also is an officer of the court, a strong-armed monitor who tries to use his muscle to see that the judge's will is done.

CONSCIENCE AND SELF-CONSCIOUSNESS

Conscience weighs the issues and conscience exerts control. Without a conscience that can make decisions and suffer from time to time as a result of decisions either wrongly made or that involve results that are not entirely pleasant, we would be no better than animals.

Charles Dickens said it well. In *David Copperfield*, he provocatively describes the indifference of his contemporaries to the heinous crime of murder. "I have seen it [indifference] displayed with such success, that I have encountered some fine ladies and gentlemen who might as well have been born caterpillars." Caterpillars, not human beings.

Conscience is the dividing line between animals and people. We human beings are not only conscious of what happens all around us—after all cats and dogs, birds and even cockroaches (I think!) have awareness. In their own ways they are conscious. But they are not *self-conscious*. They do not sit back and think about themselves. They do not measure themselves against yardsticks that enable them to judge whether they have stature in their own eyes. Only we human beings can do that.

So it is that a guilty conscience partakes in this most unique of human features: self-consciousness. Feelings are contemplated as thoughts. Pain becomes thoughts about pain. Guilt feelings become a guilty conscience, and are thereby transformed into a part of the rational mechanisms by which actions are weighed.

To be a person is, yes, to *feel* as a human being. But even more so, it is to *think* as a human being. Feeling must be transformed into thinking if we are truly to act as humans. Descartes said it on one level: I think, therefore I am. But Descartes' statement might be taken one step further: *I have a guilty conscience, therefore I am.*

CREATION AND CONSCIOUSNESS

Remember Adam and Eve. They are created and given just a few commands they are required to follow. One of them concerns forbidden fruits: "Of every tree of the garden thou mayest freely eat; but of the tree of the knowledge of good and evil, thou shalt not eat of it; for in the day that thou eatest thereof thou shalt surely die" (Genesis 2:16–17). One rule, and that rule is broken.

Before they eat of the forbidden fruit, the Bible says that they are naked and yet feel no shame (Genesis 2:25). After they eat of the forbidden fruit their eyes are opened and they perceive that they are naked. What a tremendous change: self-consciousness about the nakedness of the human body; embarrassment which makes them sew themselves loincloths. And when God calls out, asking them, "Where art thou?" Adam and Eve hide.

That is the Bible's way of saying, first of all, that self-consciousness comes from knowledge. The knowledge of distinctions, of moral rights and wrongs. It leads immediately to embarrassment, hiding, running away.

In these few verses you see the Biblical view of man, guilty by virtue of two things: having disobeyed a law, and having become self-conscious and morally aware. The combination yields a human being who wants to hide.

"The intellect," says the anonymous author of a fourteenth-century ethical work entitled *The Ways of the Righteous,* "is shame." They are one and the same thing. This author derives his sweeping assessment from the creation story, from what we know of Adam and Eve and from the transformation that takes place when they eat of the tree of knowledge.[4] In the Bible, he says, embarrassment and intelligence go hand in hand.

Benno Jacob, the twentieth-century German-Jewish Bible scholar, points out how *divine* this human embarrassment really is. In contrast to the myths of other ancient cultures, he says, Scripture nowhere speaks of God teaching man the rudiments of civilization: how to till the soil, to use fire, or to discover the wheel. These are left to man. Except for one thing: God makes leather garments for Adam and his wife (Genesis 3:21). They have nothing to do with it. And Adam and Eve do not put them on—rather, God dresses them.

All the animals were created, says Benno Jacob, happy in being their natural selves. But man? His greatest potential lay not only in his natural look, but also in a look crafted by God, a look intimately connected with human embarrassment. Only man could be embarrassed. And only man would therefore need covering.

For man was different from the rest of creation. The beautiful animals, the soaring birds, the tall giraffes, the whales, they were all exquisite creations, yet none could be embarrassed. And because none could be embarrassed, none could be self-conscious. And without self-consciousness none could ever hope to make a moral decision. Only man.

Who might develop a moral conscience, who might learn what a good deed was? Who might choose to bring glory and beauty into the world in the form of charity, in the form of kindness, in the form of morality? Only man.

Because man could be embarrassed. Because he could sense when he was wrong. His innate modesty could lead to humility. God clothed man as a sign of this special gift.[5]

WHERE HAS ALL THE CONSCIENCE GONE?

But it is a gift often shunned. For when you look around you may well wonder: Where in the world has conscience gone?

The truth is that a day rarely goes by when we do not hear of many, many people who act as if they had no conscience at all, as if a guilty conscience were not a fact of the mind but a figment of the imagination.

So many of the horrendous crimes that get into the news-papers are especially infuriating precisely because they remind us that some people have no conscience. A terrorist slaughters babies and feels proud. A swindler tries to steal your last penny when you do business with him and sheds not a tear because "that's business." A teenager stabs his neighbor because of a radio that is playing too loud. "Are you sorry for what you did?" he is asked. "Don't you think he should be punished for all that noise?" comes the response. No conscience at all.

I used to attend the lectures of a distinguished professor of international law. One day he was walking home after spending hours teaching and preparing a new book. He came to a street corner and a young thug asked him for money, then proceeded to kill this magnificent professor, a man who had stood up to the Nazis when he taught in Germany as a young man, a man who was bringing the world closer together be-cause he understood the impact of law on modern life. For dimes and quarters, for a drug fix or for kicks; it didn't matter to the killer that a life was snuffed out.

Where had conscience gone?

From time to time there are waves of corruption that fill the headlines and that batter the citizenry, making people wonder whether there is such a thing as an honest official left. One person is taking bribes, another is giving out favors with the expectation that some day he will leave government and cash in on his largesse. The brazenness is sometimes hard to fathom. Recently, for example, it was discovered that among the top ten scofflaws in New York City's Department of Transportation there are four people whose job it is to write parking tickets!

Again and again we find out that the United States Army is paying defense contractors hundreds of dollars for hammers or toilet seats. Fairness toward your country—that used to be like motherhood or apple pie. Where has conscience gone?

At the congressional Iran-Contra hearings there was a repeating theme: high officials of the government expressing a self-righteous commitment to flaunting the laws. What impressed this viewer most of all was simply the fact that the culprits had made up their minds *not to feel bad!*

The private sector, too, seems to be diseased, sick with the plagues of dishonesty and greed. Entire corporations are cited for bilking their investors or overcharging their customers. A stockbroker is called on the carpet for embezzling funds, and it turns out that whole firms are involved in check-kiting schemes.

The best and the brightest on Wall Street find new ways to make money: insider trading, it is called, a way of using privileged information to reap benefits in the stock market. Recent scandals have rocked the entire American securities industry. Business ethics, honesty, confidentiality—the question is being asked every day: Do these virtues any longer exist?

And who are the corrupt? These are not underprivileged teenagers from bad neighborhoods but the very people who have the finest educations and who are already making hundreds of thousands of dollars each year anyway—honestly.

More often than not we have a good idea where the culprits are—sunning themselves on yachts in the Caribbean, the envy of their communities because they have done so well in business and can afford the better things of life. *But where is their guilty conscience?*

Even farther away than their rapidly tanning bodies. And it has been there for eons.

THE DEACTIVATION OF CONSCIENCE

The truth is that people have abandoned their consciences for a very long time. Corruption is nothing new. About what, after all, did the prophets of Israel speak? "The wind shall feed upon all thy shepherds," said Jeremiah, "and thy lovers shall go into captivity; surely then you shall be ashamed and confounded for all thy wickedness" (Jeremiah 22:22). What caused Amos such consternation? That the rich sold the poor for a pair of shoes. What drove Isaiah to distraction? That truth and justice were abandoned as yardsticks of life. The ship of conscience has sailed on many rough seas before; ours are not its first.

You would imagine that sooner or later people would learn; and yet experience shows us that they don't.

Why? Why do people act as if there were no higher truth, no standard to which they themselves ought adhere? Why do they act as if they can do anything they want—as long as they don't get caught? Why does the booming voice of conscience frequently sound like a barely audible whisper?

Because the built-in means for sensitizing us to moral problems can be deactivated. Guilt can be shut off and the conscience drugged so that it does not do its work. The result is that the guilty conscience is put to sleep and is then often hard to wake.

At its best, guilt is a means for restoring moral balance. You want to do wrong and hopefully guilt steps in and helps to provide a corrective before the damage is actually done. Or it is a red flag after the fact, thrown down on the field to initiate a new sequence of events, frequently involving a penalty, designed to redress some wrong. That red flag is important to the game; without it the game would degenerate into a free-for-all.

But if you can convince yourself that you could not be guilty, then you won't have to worry about your conscience. And convincing arguments are not hard to find.

How do you deactivate your conscience? There are two ways

that are commonly used, two ways that cause the mind to forget about the rules of the road.

1. The first can be thought of as analogous to drunken driving. It requires a state of intellectual inebriation where the mind shuts off and only feelings (except, of course, the feelings of guilt!) remain. But this state of dangerous moral driving is not induced by a drug. Rather, it is induced by individuals, or even whole cultures, who convince themselves that guilt is *only* a feeling. They then discover themselves liberated—and we shall shortly see just how—because they no longer have to pay any attention to their minds and the guilty consciences that thoughts provoke.

This is a mental state that feels great, but a mental state that ignores rules of the road—a dangerous state which is a perfect setup for a fatal moral crash.

2. The second method doesn't drug the intellect; it plays with the mind and tries to defeat it at its very own game.

This second way to deactivate the conscience is somewhat analogous to driving with no-fault insurance. No-fault insurance enables you to collect regardless of who is to blame. But this method of deactivating your conscience works even better because it says: It is *impossible* to pin the blame on anyone. The outcome is the same, however. You don't have to pay.

This "no-fault" policy taken out on behavior uses every possible rationale to convince the mind that we should not be held responsible for the things we do. And, since we can only feel responsible for the circumstances over which we have control, this method sweet-talks the conscience and says: "Don't worry; you really don't have control over the things that happen to you. Why, then, feel responsible?"

If *we* aren't the cause of a bad situation, why then should we feel guilty? If *we* can't change the unpleasant circumstances, even were we to try, why should we feel guilty?

Two methods to undermine the conscience: let us see just how they work.

PART II
How We Try to Get Rid of Guilt and Why These Methods Do Not Work

CHAPTER 5
Moral Drunken Driving

*It really wasn't my fault, Your Honor. I
was led to believe I was above the law.*
—Joseph Farris cartoon in
The New Yorker, **April 14, 1986**

First, the way to inebriate the mind. It is possible to convince
yourself that only your feelings count. That ideas and principles
are suspect, simply because they are not feelings. And then,
happily (it is supposed), that infernal pain in the mind—the
conscience—can be put to sleep.

THE INFLATED MARKET FOR FEELINGS

Imagine, for a moment, that you are in the electronic congregation of one of America's pop preachers, the Reverend Terry
Cole-Whittaker. Naturally, you bring your conscience with you.
When you leave, however, you will be lighter and probably
happier, because you will leave your conscience behind.

People magazine describes the Reverend Cole-Whittaker's

style: "wrist-bent, head-back, molar-showing Sinatra style [that] would give a fundamentalist preacher moral jaundice."[1] The style makes use of all the emotional power the preacher has. The congregation shuts its eyes, breathes deeply, and meditates: "Pray to be released from all guilt having to do with your sexuality . . . with power and money . . . God loves you. He never judged or condemned you."

The Reverend Cole-Whittaker's good-looking, middle- and better-than-middle-class crowd exhales. Remorse, insecurity, and, of course, guilt, are cleared away.

What is her message? Love, and never, never judge. When she slips twenty-dollar bills to panhandlers, she tells them, "Don't buy food, buy booze."[2]

Don't judge. Don't even judge the Richard Specks of this world, those who murder others. His victims created their own murders, Cole-Whittaker will tell you, and Speck himself is sinless.

How can that be? It can be because, she says, we are all responsible for crime, including the crime committed against us. Not that we are all *to blame*. There is a difference between responsibility and blame. For blame implies some supreme, agreed-on moral system: Thou shalt not kill, or some variant of it. Responsibility leaves just the all-powerful individual: as victim, criminal, or self-therapist.

The conclusion: There is no right and wrong. We have to get that out of our minds. There is a vague but all-important *feeling:* the feeling of love.

Reverend Cole-Whittaker is doing very well. She has a forty-member paid staff, with another two hundred volunteers. Her organization receives more than ten thousand pieces of mail a month, and her book, *How to Have More in a Have-Not World*, has sold more than one hundred thousand copies.

Another enterprising woman, J. Z. Knight, says that a thirty-five-thousand-year-old man, Ramtha, uses her body as a channel to speak words of wisdom to her followers. Those words of wisdom are about God, who is conceived not as a remote entity but as an integral part of everything in the universe. Man, therefore, is divine, and able to create his own reality and achieve anything he desires. Freedom is achieved by abandoning one particularly old-fashioned idea, the idea of a judgmental God who, Mrs. Knight notes, you could never please. Therefore there is no sin and, of course, no guilt.

What is going on? These preachers are, of course, capitalizing on a mass phenomenon; and the wide acceptance of their ideas only scratches its surface. It is a mass appeal to feelings as the only tried-and-true way to find the good life—warm and personal feelings that unseat a cold and cruel arbiter who usually asks for a piece of the action: the mind. People trust only their feelings. They wouldn't dare trust their minds.

Even the Bible seldom regulates feelings. But when it does, it regulates them to make an important point. In the Ten Commandments, for example, only one commandment regulates feelings, and it is the most controversial of them all: "Thou shalt not covet."

The first two commandments regulate ideas: (1) the belief in God, and (2) that we shall have no other gods to which we bow down. From then on, actions are prohibited: (3) Do not take the Lord's name in vain; (4) Remember and observe the Sabbath; (5) Honor parents; (6) Thou shalt not murder; (7) Thou shalt not commit adultery; (8) Thou shalt not steal; (9) Thou shalt not bear false witness.

But the tenth commandment, Thou shalt not covet, restricts a feeling. For that reason, many of the commentators see the tenth commandment as the source of the other nine—because religion takes this level of human experience as seriously as we do in our personal lives. Feelings *are* important because they lead to ideas and actions which may be good or which may be bad. But feelings do not exist all by themselves.

You are not allowed to covet because coveting your neighbor's wife could lead to adultery; coveting his ox could lead to theft. Both of these could lead to murder. Lusts of the heart of various kinds could lead to an attraction to other gods. You see the approach. Therefore feelings are regulated.

But the pop preachers and the masses of people who are primed for their message don't want to think about where feelings could lead. They don't want to imagine that greed could lead to insider trading or bilking the government; that lust can lead to adultery and that adultery can destroy marriages, families, and lives.

Only the feelings count. And that is true about guilt, too. Feelings of guilt should lead to ideas about what is correct to do or not to do. But that connection never happens when only feelings count.

If guilt is *only* a feeling, then morals are entirely a private affair. If guilt is *only* a feeling, then it raises no issues that are likely to need public examination. If anything, guilt will raise highly private matters which will have to do only with *how good you feel*.

That is one of the reasons why it seems so preposterous to dwell on guilt. Why all we want is for someone to tell us only *how to get rid of guilt* because guilt is a bad feeling and we do not want to feel bad.

THE PUBLIC PILLORY

In a feeling culture, what does it take to make a conscience guilty these days? When it is at all possible, it takes the modern form of a public pillory: a lot of headlines; perhaps a public hearing. It takes the transformation of a private deed into a public event. Suddenly, then, the possibility of a guilty conscience.

Before that, it was all personal. The politician may have assumed that kickbacks were a good way to raise his standard of living. His expenses are great. He has to keep up his house and his family, and why should he, too, not reap some of the material benefits of modern life: a country home, a nice car? No one is getting hurt.

Then he gets caught. These private doings suddenly become public and wear the garments of morality for the first time. *Where was his conscience before that?* It was a *private* matter, and private matters do not breed consciences; they only breed happiness or sadness or other *feelings*—not morals or standards, which, by definition, are beyond each individual.

The attitude is not unusual. Is it not a byword of modern

living that a person should be true to himself, that his feelings are reliable guides to his behavior and that any interference into his moral sphere by standards that exist beyond himself is an interference with the most personal and private side of his life? Morals are, therefore, beyond the pale as subjects of reasonable debate. The goal is, rather, self-discovery, freeing the individual from the constraints of outside systems or rules.

But you can't have much of a conscience if all you ever do is *talk to yourself.* Such narcissistic self-reliance, where our only reference points are internal, is partially responsible for the fact that conscience seems to be in such short supply.

THE MYTH OF MORAL THERAPY

In a book entitled *The Myth of Neurosis: Overcoming the Illness Excuse*, psychologist Garth Wood advocates an approach to psychology which he calls "Moral Therapy" and which illustrates quite well the pitfalls of plumbing your own feelings and expecting to find enlightenment only there.

Dr. Wood, too, is allergic to rules. So allergic, in fact, that he would reject even those rules that may seem good, and which we may want to integrate into our lives. "Never must we try to force any set rules onto either a willing or an unwilling recipient," he says.[3] Rather, moral therapy liberates us from rules so that we can discover ourselves and become truly free.

Now Dr. Wood is not opposed to conscience, but to him conscience is something you and I can know only by plumbing the depths of our inner selves. And, since there are no rules of the road, the journey can lead anywhere. And wherever it does lead is, by definition, good. There "conscience" is to be found.

If, for example, your conscience leads you to violent acts, then be led there, even to be a terrorist. *As long as it is good for you.* Dr. Wood writes:

> I have examined this rather harrowing example to emphasize the vital point that Moral Therapy does not seek to lay down general moral laws. It has no ax to grind, no propaganda to make. It is not in the business of exporting ready-

made codes that it would urge others to accept. It is rather a process of discovery in which the codes of others are analyzed, so that they can benefit from a closer obedience to their *own* unique disciplinary systems.[4]

Self-discovery. Uniqueness. These are the bywords of the search. Bywords of a search carried on exclusively with reference to one's feelings. Do you think conscience will be found here?

What of the unique and strongly held consciences of Adolf Hitler and his cohorts who felt that the world would be much better off without any Jews? What of Josef Stalin, that "conscientious" man who felt so strongly about his enemies that he had them all killed? Or of Pol Pot and his moralistic revolution that killed millions of innocent human beings? Or of those who murder because they find the experience elevating or thrilling or simply useful? Follow your conscience, right?

The truth is that a definition of conscience which sees it as unique and personal is no definition of conscience at all. We have personal feelings, no doubt. But matters of conscience are, first and foremost, matters that go beyond our feelings and that place us before codes of behavior that, heaven forfend, we may be obligated to serve.

Dr. Wood is afraid of what he calls "the Nuremberg factor." He is afraid that people will be willing to abandon their consciences to do whatever the authorities tell them to do. And here it is easy to agree with Dr. Wood. But he goes on to write: "If we are to avoid the Nuremberg factor, we would do well to admit the supremacy of personal moral imperatives and to follow faithfully, through thick and thin, the commands of our own unique ethical systems wherever they may lead us."[5]

May we be saved from such systems! This entire point of view is based on the certainty that unique feelings are absolutely reliable guides for human action. Guides, yes—but such guides are far from being absolutely reliable. Feelings need to be weighed against something else.

If feelings are not subject to the scrutiny of the mind, then the emotions of lust and greed may control the human being.

THE POWER OF RATIONALIZATION

And do not forget the capacity that people have to rationalize their feelings. It is an awesome process to watch and it teaches us quickly to be wary about what we tell ourselves.

Clergymen are exposed to the process of rationalization all the time. I love to hear the reasons why people didn't come to services last week. And I am even more fascinated by the two sides presented by a married couple riven with strife.

We all rationalize, and people always have. For years, great thinkers have been sensitive to such pitfalls of the human psyche. What a pity if their insights are forgotten today.

Back in the eleventh century, for example, there was a Spanish-Jewish philosopher named Rabbi Bahya ibn Paquda who wrote a book on spirituality entitled *The Duties of the Heart.* One of his chapters is entitled "Taking Stock," and is devoted to an examination of introspection. Rabbi Bahya points out that introspection is one of the world's most difficult tasks—difficult because we rationalize and convince ourselves that our feelings are our best guides.

Bahya notes that even our efforts to be good may be infused with a variety of motives—such as a desire to further our own agendas or to impress others with our righteousness. What we really want is to *feel* pride. And we may therefore convince ourselves that a hundred different actions are praiseworthy because they inflate our pride.

THERE OUGHT TO BE A LAW

Conscience must base itself on something *outside* of the individual. It is nothing if it is not based on a *law.* You may want to steal that gold watch you have always coveted; you may want to forget about the obligations you have to your family; you may want to destroy anyone who gets in your way. Why not do it?

Because it is a matter of conscience.

Because intuitively we feel that there is a law which says *No!* That is the only reason not to do it. Because it is not right, whether we like it or not. Whether we find it fulfilling or not. It doesn't matter one whit. Because *there is a law!*

Conscience forces us to confront *intuitive* realities without which we cannot live responsibly and without which we cannot expect to behave morally. For every measurement we make assumes the presence of some yardstick that stands behind it. Look at the way guilt works.

You feel guilty because you do not give as much charity as you should? Your conscience points you toward a higher principle: concern for others and the need to share one's material well-being. You feel guilty because you do not allow your wife to pursue her own interests and create her own role? Your conscience points you toward the powerful rights that every individual has and the need of all of us to support and relate to the personal autonomy of everyone who is near and dear to us. You assume that people should feel guilty if they cheat on their taxes or embezzle money from their employers or steal gold chains from women walking to work? Your conscience points you toward the need we have to respect other people's integrity, to respect their possessions as well as their rights. You assume that people should feel guilty if they gun down innocent passengers on airplanes in the name of one political cause or another? Your conscience points you toward the truth that every human being is sacred and should not be used as a means toward an end.

Feelings engendered by guilt push ordinary people—not only philosophers, mind you, but ordinary, sensitive people—to become believers. Not necessarily believers in the rituals of one faith or another. But confronting situations that are pregnant with meaning forces us to posit, with whatever doubts necessary, that we cannot make a move and that we cannot organize a rational response to moral questions without using a yardstick, a law, that we try to ascertain to the best of our abilities. One of the interesting anomalies of the guilty conscience is that it places most of us in the position of acting *as if* there were a right and a wrong, as uncomfortable as such an idea may make us modern people feel.

The intellect measures rights and wrongs; it assesses our actions against these unwritten laws. Therefore the very metaphors used for sin and guilt convey the sense that one "misses the mark" when doing wrong. In Hebrew, for example, the word for sin is *het*, which means, very simply, "missing the mark." Other words are commonly used: error, for example, comes from the Latin *errare*, to wander. "Deviation," "transgression," these are all locational metaphors that indicate the assumption that there is a mark, a path, a line to follow, and the sinner goes astray if he does not follow it.

"The heavens declare the glory of God," Psalm 19 states, and the psalm goes on to speak about the wonder of the firmament. Several verses later, however, a transition is made from praising God for the beauties of creation to praising the Lord for His law. "The law of the Lord is perfect, restoring the soul: the testimony of the Lord is sure, making wise the simple./ The precepts of the Lord are right, rejoicing the heart: the commandment of the Lord is pure, enlightening the eyes" (Psalms 19:8–9).

The very religious sensitivity that turns a person to the world and leads him to praise the glory of God for its creation turns the morally aware and spiritually searching human being above and beyond himself to the law of God.

GUILT IS MORE THAN SOMETHING INSIDE

Granted, these steps that lift us out of our selves and into the larger world of the spirit are hard steps to take—hard steps for each of us, since they go so much against the grain. Robert Coles, the Harvard psychologist, has written that he himself faced a similar predicament when, with difficulty, he overcame this predisposition to see only feelings and not the larger issues that guilt reveals.[6]

A woman came to see him, racked by guilt. As a highly skilled person, Dr. Coles had the tools, he thought, to understand this patient's guilt. Both his education and mode of thinking had taught him that guilt was the manifestation of unconscious inner drives. Therefore, when this woman came to see him suffering from depression, he used his psychiatric knowledge to try to discover the unconscious sources of her irrational behavior.

Note how he was predisposed: to react to her troubles as if

they were the result of some highly personal, unique feelings—feelings so personal that they were likely to be unconscious. *Guilt was only a feeling.*

She, on the other hand, spoke to him about more conscious concerns: a specific deed she had committed, a sexual liaison with her employer, and about the remorse she felt as a result. The doctor, however, was taught that such a feeling must be an outer manifestation of "something deeper." Dr. Coles's supervisor at a hospital suggested that the woman's guilt was based on the connection made in her own mind between the man with whom she had slept and her father.

The woman didn't agree. She persisted, against the better judgment of the psychiatrist. " 'You keep trying to find the cause of my difficulty within me,' she said, 'but I believe there's someone else who has to be mentioned.' " That someone else, to the psychiatrist's chagrin, turned out to be God. The woman felt she had committed a transgression. As she put it: "It is sin I'm talking about."

Dr. Coles remembers asking this intelligent woman what "sin" had to do with her moods. He thought to himself that perhaps she was sicker than he had first realized and that she had resorted to religious terminology to avoid discussing painful psychological matters. Her response to him was pointed: "God's judgment matters more than my own."

Dr. Coles concludes finally: "I didn't have the courage and integrity to tell my supervisor, tell myself, how helpful it had been for that patient, for me as well, to have the discussion we'd had, to think about (assisted by another person) what is right and wrong in the largest moral perspective possible."[7]

What Dr. Coles learned is that guilt is more than a feeling. Because it is more than a feeling, it asks questions, it raises issues, it makes claims. It produces a conscience that is alive and well, and it prods that conscience. If guilt were only a feeling, then there would be nothing to say beyond "Are you feeling good?" But there is more to life than that!

An appeal to conscience is an appeal with meaning precisely because it is *not* an appeal to anyone's private feelings but to something that it is assumed can and should be accepted *by all*.

But since only feelings have come to be our guides, is it any wonder that we have ever so many people without a conscience? Feelings, as integral a part of us as they may be, are no foundation upon which a towering conscience can be built.

The first reason why conscience is in such short supply is related, then, to our propensity to see only our feelings as our guides. Guilt is more than a feeling, and if we deny its power as an idea, then we do not recognize how much our minds can teach us about the right way to live.

But there is a second reason why the guilty conscience is so often absent: the ever-present suspicion we have that *we* are not in charge of our lives and therefore that *we* are not responsible for what we do. If we are not responsible, then of course we cannot be guilty. And we will never bear the burden of living with a guilty conscience.

Let us see, next, how this process works.

CHAPTER 6
Don't Blame Me!

This is the excellent foppery of the world, that, when we are sick in fortune, —often the surfeits of our own behaviour,—we make guilty of our disasters the sun, the moon, and stars, as if we were villains on necessity, fools by heavenly compulsion, knaves, thieves, and treachers by spherical predominance, drunkards, liars, and adulterers by an enforc'd obedience of planetary influence. . . .
—William Shakespeare, *King Lear*

And now at this point in the meeting I'd like to shift the blame away from me and onto someone else.
—Michael Maslin cartoon in
The New Yorker, August 19, 1985

Who is in charge of our lives? Who makes the important decisions, the ones that determine whether we are bad or good, nasty or kind? Who determines the crucial features of our character? Do we do it ourselves or is it done for us by someone else, or by something else over which we have no control?

These questions have preoccupied mankind from ancient

times until our own. Among the philosophers of Greece, for example, many wondered what it meant for man to be free. These thinkers understood that every action is the result of a long list of other actions, or causes, that precede it in time. If I take a swing at my neighbor, for example, it is very unlikely that my swing is entirely spontaneous. My own history, the history of our relationship, all are a part of what seems like a free action. Could we say that *these factors* cause me to swing? Can we speak of ourselves as being free and responsible agents when so much history goes into every action we take?

If the cause of our wrongdoing lies outside of ourselves, then we cannot have a guilty conscience. Someone else is responsible, not us. Some set of circumstances is responsible, not us. And there is a wide variety of possibilities when it comes to finding someone else to blame for the people we know as ourselves.

THE RELIGIOUS EXCUSE

Some people blame God. They feel they are very pious by assuming that God is in charge, that He does absolutely everything according to His will and that we are therefore puppets who move our arms and our legs because of the divine strings that are attached to them.

Such a view is particularly attractive to those religions that grow out of the Bible, religions that believe in a God who is all-powerful and all-knowing. The historian of philosophy Harry A. Wolfson describes the numerous thinkers who have seen everything as being in God's hands as "predestinarians," that is, they believe that everything is predetermined by an all-knowing and all-powerful God.

Muslim philosophers, basing their beliefs on verses of the Koran, formulated a doctrine of human action based on predestinarian views. While an alternative view that advocated man's freedom began to grow toward the end of the seventh century in the schools of the Kadariyyah and later in those of the Mu'tazillites, nonetheless the predisposition to assume that events will take place "if Allah wills it" has characterized Islam.[1]

Christians have had their Calvin to teach that all actions are predetermined. And Judaism, too, has had its thinkers such as Hasdai ibn-Crescas in the fifteenth century, and the Hasidic Rabbi Joseph of Isbesz, who maintain that because of God's foreknowledge man is not really free.

It may seem pious, but it is a dangerous idea. First, think of all the horrendous immoral acts committed over the ages in the name of faith. Then, think of the insane individuals who commit atrocities and claim God as their guide. But beyond this, the puppeteering God undermines the Bible itself.

In the Middle Ages, Maimonides attacked all those who had such a faith by soberly pointing out that *each person* is in charge of his own life. The Scriptures, he points out, presuppose human free will. They are filled with exhortations which make no sense if people cannot choose. Of course, a "person may be so constituted to find it easy or hard to do a certain thing." But that things are predetermined "is absolutely untrue." [2]

If God pulls all the strings, then the Bible makes no sense. Which is not to say that God is responsible for nothing. He contributes, but *He does not control.* He pulls some of those strings. He has created the world. He has created the facts of nature as well as many of the facts of life that are beyond our control.

But who is in charge? Man is in charge of his own life, and therefore there is guilt.

THE GENETIC EXCUSE

But God is not the only scapegoat. Some people say that our behavior is beyond our control because *it is all in the genes.* You are what you are. You are made in a certain way, biologically and psychologically, and that's that. Whether you are prone to anger or are phlegmatic, whether you are prone to beneficence or are miserly, it is all in the genes. If you do right or if you do wrong, it is because you are made that way and anatomy is destiny; physiology determines psychology. Even if God doesn't pull the strings, it is all preordained.

Many people believe this. Remember that one of the growth businesses these days is a new kind of bank, the "sperm bank."

You go there to make yourself a Nobel prize-winning child, made by the logical recipe of using a Nobel prizewinner's sperm. Such banks are stocked with genius material, all with the hope of producing a generation of future Einsteins.

There is good logic behind this. If our behavior is a product of drives, and if drives have their sources in biochemical substances, then the right route to perfection is through the propper manipulation of these substances.

Now if it is all in the genes, what can you do about the person you are? You find it impossible to control the feelings of anger you have toward your terrible two-year-old? You are an angry person and therefore others, including your child, should beware before crossing your path? Feel guilty? For what? You have no choice—your genes are talking and you are only being yourself!

Your libidinal sexual drives are great, and there seems to be no way to resist the temptation of a beautiful woman in the right circumstances. Isn't it natural to stray? Feel guilty? For what? You are being yourself!

Should you feel guilty for the genes you received? That is your parents' burden, not your own. Let them feel guilty for the genes they have given you. For you, however, there is freedom from guilt.

This biological predetermination can take less radical forms as well. Recently the Prime Minister of Great Britain, Margaret Thatcher, used a variation on this theme. When asked whether she might change what were to the questioner some of the objectionable sides of her character, she replied with prime ministerly aplomb, "I cannot be objective enough to see myself the way others see me. The only thing I can say is that I am too old to change."

Too old to change. Once again there are objective circumstances written into the physiological constitution of a human being which preclude the possibility of having control over one's own moral destiny. Who is in charge? Always someone or something else.

Genes obviously contribute, age is a factor in behavior, and there is undoubtedly a chemical predisposition to certain types of behavior which each of us uniquely possesses. But *they do not control.*

THE ENVIRONMENTAL EXCUSE

And if, finally, it isn't all in the genes, then perhaps our behavior can be understood entirely *because of the environment.* Why does a criminal steal or murder, for example? Because of the environment. Why are we unkind to our husbands and our wives? Because of our childhoods. Aren't we all products of our environments?

I was a student of the late B. F. Skinner, and I shall never forget the glee in Skinner's eyes as he trained a pigeon in front of the class. He had kept the pigeon hungry, and he began to feed it only when it turned its head backwards. In no time at all, the pigeon was turning somersaults, the goal the professor had in mind right from the start. Skinner went on from there to teach that behavior is a complex product of stimulus-response reactions. The bottom line was this: that the environment controls the behavior of an animal. And from there, how easy it is to conclude that the environment controls a human being.

The environment obviously contributes, but *it does not control.* A bad childhood? That makes for a tough road that an individual will have to walk, for that person may have weaknesses that will make it easy for him to fall. You and I need to have sympathy for him, to help him overcome his environmentally conditioned bad behavior. We will have sympathy also for his tumbles, since mercy becomes us as human beings.

But if we were to then decide that a person is not responsible for what he does, we would be creating an environmental crisis worse than any produced by PCBs (industrial pollutants of waterways). We would be pulling away the rug of human dignity on which we are privileged to walk. The environment would become an alibi instead of an aid in our understanding of what makes people tick. It would become the environmental excuse. It would tell us that *we are not in charge and that we cannot be held responsible for what we do.*

Not in charge because of God. Not in charge because of our genes. Not in charge because of our environment. *Not in charge.*

But a guilty conscience reminds us of one of the most important, yet unpleasant, of human facts: You *are* in charge of your life. Though God does play a part, still *you are in charge*. Though the genes set up a group of personality predispositions, still *you are in charge*. Though the environment has a powerful effect upon behavior, still *you are in charge*. You need to be ready and willing to take responsibility for your deeds.

Who is ready to do that? We prefer to blame someone else, over and over again. Just as Adam and Eve did. After they eat of the forbidden fruit, God confronts them with the wrongness of what they have done. What does Adam say? Eve told me to do it. What does Eve say? It was the serpent's fault. And who is blamed? All three. For each of them had a responsible part in the irresponsible action. All three are therefore blamed.

REASON IS RESPONSIBLE

If the bottom line is responsibility, then, how do you take charge of your life? By putting *your mind* to it. By using your intellect to maintain control.

Maimonides, in his study of human psychology, notes that there is a variety of factors that influence behavior. In the philosophical language of his time he spoke of these factors as the *faculties of the soul*. We would probably call them the physical and psychological sources that motivate human behavior.[3]

These faculties take into account the biological necessities, the physical drives. They include the emotions and the imagination. But sitting above them all is one human faculty that is in charge: *reason*, the human mind.

With reason in charge, every human being is free, to a very great extent, to control his own life—not to make himself taller or shorter, but to raise or lower his stature nonetheless. Not to choose his allotment of brains, but to make use of the gifts he has received. Not to choose the parents that are to give him birth, but to choose what to do with the infinite number of natural endowments he has received.

His behavior and ultimately his happiness are in no one else's hands but his own. He must, however, make choices. And to know what choices to make, he must develop his reason to the fullest possible extent.

The intellect, therefore, is not only the nerve center but the control center of the moral human being. Conscience is the element that exerts rational control. It is the center's chief operating officer. Its duty is to make the tough decisions. Because the buck stops here.

Therefore, do not be afraid to sit back and think about your behavior. Those thoughts are the key to your control. They can shed the light that can pierce the darkness, that can bring new direction to your life. Not by themselves, perhaps, but they are the starting place.

FEELING AND THOUGHT

Feeling guilty. A guilty conscience. What we have seen up until now is a reminder of the two-sided nature of human life, recognized since antiquity, but perpetually a problem in every age. Man is a combination of feeling and thought, of emotions and intellect. And when we begin to uncover the many layers of a concept as seemingly simple as guilt, we see that guilt itself is a product of these two separate but united sides of human life.

Feeling guilty is the beginning. Feeling guilty is the source of powerful behaviors and of the deepest levels motivating change. A guilty conscience is both the outward manifestation of feelings and the arbiter that involves the mind in controlling the emotions, and is therefore the central locus for moral activity in human life.

Guilt that is emotional and intellectual is therefore *a desirable necessity of human existence,* abandoned only at the peril of abandoning everything that is worthwhile in our lives.

But guilt doesn't have to be abandoned. Not when it makes sense and is appropriate. The real problem with guilt is not that it is inherently bad, but that we often feel guilty when we should not—that we are blamed for something we didn't do.

Let us take a look at those circumstances which we truly haven't created, those that are beyond our control.

CHAPTER 7
Due to Circumstances Beyond Our Control

The name of the angel who is in charge of conception is Laylah. He takes up a drop and places it in the presence of the Holy One, blessed be He, saying: O Lord of the universe, what is in store for this drop? Is it destined to produce a strong man or a weak man, a wise man or a foolish man, a rich man or a poor man? He does not, however, inquire whether it is to produce a wicked man or a righteous man. It thus bears out the view of R. Hanina, for R. Hanina said: "Everything is in the power of Heaven except the fear of Heaven."
—**Talmud,** *Nidah* 16b

Holding firmly to the trunk, I took a step toward him, and then my knees bent and I jounced the limb. Finny, his balance gone, swung his head around to look at me for an instant with extreme interest,

> *and then he tumbled sideways, broke*
> *through the little branches below and hit*
> *the bank with a sickening unnatural*
> *thud.*
> —**John Knowles**, *A Separate Peace*

From time to time, television programs are interrupted and, for a short while, you wonder what the source of the problem is: your television set or the broadcast itself. Often, then, an announcement appears on the screen which reads something like "Due to circumstances beyond our control, there will be a short delay in the transmission of this program." I, for one, always breathe a sigh of relief, for it means the problem is with someone or something else and not with my set.

Then I wonder: Are the circumstances really beyond their control, or has the station resorted to a clever ruse to make sure that I and others will not be able to pin any blame on them? It was a crucial video message: "Due to circumstances beyond our control . . ." for guilt and control go together. When you are in control, you have responsibility. When you have responsibility, you can have guilt.

But what if you really lack control? What if you are feeling guilty for something that you really could not have caused, nor could you have prevented it from happening? Should you still feel guilty just because you are part of a scenario that involves someone's suffering—even when the events are due to circumstances beyond your control?

Not at all.

Take the case of an elderly woman who has just fallen and suffered a broken hip. She is beside herself—not only because she is now bedridden. Her elderly husband is completely dependent on her for cooking his meals and for taking care of the necessities of his life. Lying in her hospital bed, the woman doesn't pity herself. She weeps to her son who has come to visit her: "Look what I have done to your father. All because I forgot to take my cane when I went over to the cupboard, look what I have done to him!"

Now it doesn't take long for her son to start generating his own guilt. He thinks: I should have hired someone to help my mother in the house by now. She really can't take care of herself, let alone my father. If I hadn't spent my money on the down payment for our country house, I could have at least paid for someone for a little while. And, who knows? That little while could have prevented her dreadful fall. Had she not fallen, both she and my father would be getting along quite well now. It is all my fault.

Can you see what is going on here? Guilt. Great gobs of guilt. Each person is so aware of his or her own responsibilities that no one has to remind them of Adam and Eve to say: Take responsibility! Don't hide! A failure to take responsibility is not the problem.

Someone has to remind them, though, that elderly women often have osteoporosis—a condition about which we have only recently acquired medical knowledge (and thus the elderly woman would not have known how to prevent it). As a result of osteoporosis, breaking a hip is commonly not the result of a fall, but the cause of the fall itself. It is very likely that this woman would have broken her hip had she had her cane in hand or not. And her son would not have been able to prevent the fall either, had there been a caretaker on the premises or not. What they all have to remember is that the fall was *due to circumstances beyond their control*, and when that is the case, it is inappropriate to place any blame.

Who should feel guilty about the woman's fall? No one, no one at all. They should spend their energy trying to cope with the real problems of dealing with illness in old age, and they should save themselves the wear and tear caused by turning this unfortunate set of circumstances into a guilt trip.

THE BAD NEWS AND THE GOOD NEWS TOO

In Chapter 6, responsibility seemed to be the bad news—bad news since it meant that human beings had to be willing to take responsibility for their actions and consequently to suffer pangs of guilt as a result of doing wrong. Now you see that fixing responsibility is not all bad. To the contrary, here is the good news: You shouldn't feel guilty when there is insufficient reason for you to feel that way. Cross-examine the guilt. Let it check out the facts. The crucial question to ask yourself is: Are your actions (or even your inactions) the cause of the problem? Are they even a significant contributing cause? Or is this situation one in which, in all truth, unfortunate developments have materialized which are "due to circumstances beyond your control"?

If you analyze what is happening, you will quickly see that so many guilt-ridden situations shouldn't make you feel guilty at all. Or at least they shouldn't make you feel *as* guilty as you feel.

Remember—letting down the people you love will make you feel guilty. That is how it should be. But at the same time, precisely because you love your mother and because you love your husband, your guilt feelings are likely to spring into action just the way the U.S. government's early-warning system guards against nuclear attacks. A plane is always in the air, ready to go. So it is with guilt, which is always there to help protect someone you love. Your backup emotions are all set to take off at the slightest sign, and before you even know it you will witness a full-scale guilt attack.

The only way to know whether this is a real or a false alarm, however, is to base your feelings on the best intelligence reports. The mind is the best antidote. Let it cross-examine the guilt; let it check out the facts. Are you responsible or are you not? The verdict may very well be: Not guilty at all!

SUPERGUILT

Women are particularly susceptible to "mother's guilt," and in this day of superwomen it is commonly also "superguilt." Every mother has a little bit at least some of the time. But so often it is an inappropriate guilt to feel. Lynn Caine wrote a thoughtful exposé of the way in which mothers are being blamed for everything in her book *What Did I Do Wrong? Mothers, Children, Guilt.*[1] Her message to the mothers of America is refreshingly blunt: "Stop blaming yourself."

Is it ever appropriate for mothers to feel guilty, she asks? Certainly it is. If you "beat the hell out of your crying baby— then, yes, guilt is appropriate. But if your kid does foolish, self-destructive things—and what kid doesn't?—why assume that you're responsible? How are kids going to learn anything if they don't make mistakes? Guilt stems from a failure to understand that there are many factors that influence how a child turns out —genes, intelligence, position in the family, looks, economics and luck."[2]

Caine is right. Mothers have to be particularly careful that they do not do themselves damage by feeling guilty for innumerable things over which they have no control. Ask yourself: Are these circumstances my doing, or are these problems due to circumstances beyond my control? And remember, there are many things such as genes, intelligence, fate, and the world outside over which no one has control. That doesn't mean that problems will not happen. It just means that you can save yourself a great deal of guilt some of the time.

And this is especially true for working mothers, who are in an ideal situation for magnifying even the smallest of feelings of guilt. Cartoonist Gary Trudeau, husband of television's Jane Pauley (herself the consummate working mom), pictured the position of the working mother very poignantly in one of his Doonesbury comic strips. A child is being picked up from a day-care center, and he tells his mother, "I was crying because all the other children went home and you were late again, but Mrs. Wicker gave me Oreos and let me watch cartoons and I called her 'Mommy' by mistake." The mother looks at the child and says, "You play hardball, kid."

In any situation conducive to guilt you have to be especially on your guard. Not to never feel guilty—because sometimes you should. But often you should not. Remember the question: Have I really caused the unfortunate outcome so that I should feel guilty as a result?

Working mothers so often have multiple agendas that do not easily balance. They, and usually their husbands, juggle many responsibilities and maintain a careful balancing act. By and large, most people do an extraordinary job and are able to achieve numerous goals: family, work, and even communal concerns. But there is still a battle that has to be waged against feeling guilty for insufficient reason.

Beware of those people who will use guilt to make you feel bad, even though they have good intentions. In an article directed at working women, Gloria Norris and Joann Miller warn against some dangerous people who are out to get working women. Among them the authors mention "grandmother guilt" and "doctor guilt."[3]

Take grandmother guilt. Mothers and mothers-in-law often become protectors of their grandchildren. They see themselves as combining the infallible wisdom of experience with the rational, objective judgment of distance. If the disapproving grandmother baby-sits for you, she has a double stranglehold. First, there is the martyrdom of doing what she feels should be your job. "My daughter works, so I keep her children," these willing do-gooders sigh to friends. Second, she becomes the expert on your child—and you can be sure she'll report all the bad news.

One young woman, returning to graduate school at twenty-nine, asked her mother to take over at home. To her distress, "When I'd get home, my mother would say, 'Jonathan has been sitting at the door waiting for you for the past hour.' Maybe he was, but she should have been doing something to amuse him. Of course, I didn't see it that way for a long time. She made me feel guilty as hell."

Doctors, Norris and Miller note, are just a notch below grandparents in their power to induce guilt in us. This doesn't mean that they shouldn't caution you about times when a baby might be especially vulnerable to your absence, or suggest that your child seems sad or lonely. But if all you hear is disapproval, if your pediatrician routinely doles out guilt along with the medical advice, switch doctors—these authors rightly say.

Even the psychiatrists don't come away without a scratch. One couple discovered this when they went to see a psychiatrist about their six-year-old son's fear of going to school. The doctor, a child psychoanalyst with a distinguished reputation, immediately labeled the boy's problem "school phobia," a serious disorder, and then proceeded to question only the child's mother. When she mentioned that she had returned to work a few months before, the doctor leaned back in his chair with the air of a detective who had cornered his prey.

"With school phobia," the doctor explained patiently, "we look to the mother. With arson," he added, turning to the boy's father for the first time, "we look to the father." "I see," said the father, "and whom do you look to if the child wants to burn down the school?"

Understandably disenchanted, the couple decided to take matters into their own hands. It turned out that their boy was frightened of his teacher, whose bantering, aggressive style didn't suit this child's shy nature. A meeting with the principal, a change in teachers, a few days of Daddy lingering in the new classroom—and the "school phobia" was cured.

In each of these cases a working mother found herself feeling guilty for specific problems which she didn't cause. Rather, other people, those who disapproved of her working, interpreted the facts in ways that gave them ammunition to use. But their ammunition, alas, was aimed at an undeserving foe.

Undoubtedly, the more problems there are, the more possibilities for guilt there are as well. Parents of schizophrenic children, for example, feel a tremendous amount of guilt—but here, too, often for insufficient reason. Because so much behavior is environmental in origin, they assume that their children's problems are totally the result of something that they have done. Yet more and more research shows us that while a child's environment may exacerbate a congenital predisposition to schizophrenia, physiological brain dysfunction is the primary culprit. In many instances, the schizophrenia is due to circumstances beyond the parents' control. Ponder the scientific facts before inflicting yourself with guilt.[4]

Families of people who commit suicide are plagued with terrible, terrible guilt. What could we have done, they ask themselves interminably, to insure that the suicide never would have taken place? There are, perhaps, missed opportunities that will be recalled. And, indeed, therapy will be very helpful for enabling a family to work out what might have been done, and what could not have been anticipated at all. But the temptation is to feel saddled with guilt and to crumble under that burden. It is wise and even necessary to remember how complicated individual human beings are, and how many unpleasant features of other people's behaviors—even our own children's—are beyond our control.

The bottom line is this: Don't feel guilty when you are not likely to be the cause of a problem. Ask that question: Have I caused the problem? Is the circumstance one over which I have control, and would I do something different if I could? And don't be afraid of the fact that you will never be completely sure whether perhaps you have more control than you think. The chances are that you will never know for sure—that you will have to go with your instincts.

But go with them. Use your gut as well as your head to establish whether you bear any fault.

KNOWING TOO MUCH

Guilt presumes a cause-and-effect relationship. If you cause something, then you could feel guilty if it turns out to be harmful or bad. Establishing the nexus between cause and effect that defines responsibility is particularly important nowadays.

We are part of an expanding world of knowledge, a world in which we have more and more pieces of information and in which we often assume that we understand all the causes for everything that happens: Why people get sick or are healthy, for example. We even assume that death is within our control, and that if we do everything just right, then death, too, will be defeated. Because we often do have more control, there are more occasions for feeling guilty. But the truth is that we don't control as much as we think.

Russell Baker, the humorist, recently bemoaned this state of affairs. "As the years passed," he writes, "it became increasingly obvious that if I died it would be my own fault. This saddened me. . . .

"When I die I want people to commiserate. . . . Lately, though, when it looks as if you may be in a mortal pickle, what you're more likely to hear is: 'Tough buns, sweetheart. If you'd watched your cholesterol, exercised an hour a day, stuffed down more fiber, supplemented your calcium intake and popped a daily aspirin, you wouldn't be spoiling everybody's day with the death rattle. . . . The new theory is, you brought it on yourself, so don't expect any sympathy from me, Buster.' "[5]

This view is an interesting side effect of too much preventive medicine: guilt. You feel that you could have avoided the circumstances—yet in reality you could not. The effects are debilitating.

When a person is sick, for example, the thought that he is responsible for his illness can be a source of further pain. So writes the author and journalist Paul Cowan in a moving article on his own life as a patient fighting cancer. Cowan won many battles in that fight, though he eventually lost the war.

During the first weeks of his treatment, he read books by many different kinds of healers, those who believed in psychological healing, as well as those who believed in the power of diet and yoga to affect his fight against the dread disease he had. Yet he balked at the underlying assumption these writers made:

> They agree that there is a psychological cause for sickness. Indeed, Dr. Bernie S. Siegel, the influential author of the best-selling *Love, Medicine and Miracles,* argues that there is a "cancer personality" and describes its characteristic traits at length. Furthermore, these writers argue, there is a correct psychological pathway back to health. . . .
>
> But I also have to confront the awesome mysterious power of my disease. Otherwise, if the leukemic cells reenter my bone marrow, I run the risk of blaming myself for relapsing and, if I continue to weaken, of raging at my psyche instead of fighting back.[6]

Cowan is right. While they are undoubtedly trying to help, the many writers that give guidance to restoring health can also undermine a person's sense of integrity by making him feel guilty for being ill. Because we know so much about medicine, we must be on guard lest we think that we know it all.

Sometimes you should feel guilty. If you are eating foods that are known to cause heart conditions, for example. If you are smoking so that you increase your susceptibility to lung cancer or to heart disease. If you engage in I.V. drug use or sexual practices that are well known to spread AIDS. You should feel guilty when you have done these things, and the guilt may help you to help yourself and to change a habit that may kill you in the end.

But all that having been said, there are other conditions over which you cannot have any control. Before you feel guilty, ask yourself: Have I really caused the unfortunate outcome so that I should feel as guilty as I do?

There is nothing sacred or holy about feeling bad. Feeling guilty may be a useful feeling when it helps to clarify the dimensions of moral problems we face day in and day out. Feeling guilty is a tool in the workshop of moral living, one that has to be used well or else it can cause injury rather than be a help in the crafting of our lives. And because guilt is more than a feeling, because it operates in conjunction with our intelligence, then a fair amount of careful thought is called for if we are to benefit from guilt.

If you shouldn't be feeling guilty, reason with yourself and do your best to listen to what reason says. Your feelings have ears, and they can respond to what you say to yourself.

On the other hand, you may find yourself rightly blamed. In that case, don't deny the guilty feelings but learn how to use them. For, strange as it may seem, the purpose of guilt is not to make you feel bad, but to make you feel good. A paradox? Not at all—as we shall see once we get a better idea of just how guilt works.

PART III
The Ways in Which Guilt Can Debilitate Us and How We Can Fight Back

CHAPTER 8
Feeling Good

*There is no greater guilt than
discontentment.*
—*The Way of Lao-Tzu*, **46**

*I wish I could feel better about feeling
good.*
—**Comedian Richard Lewis**

Sometimes, strange as it may seem, feeling bad is a stepping-stone to feeling good.

The embezzler who was in search of his soul felt guilty, but his guilt had as its ultimate purpose the goal of feeling good. The woman who had lost her husband—she, too, was finding out something about herself which, while painful, was eventually going to enable her to feel better. The man with a guilty conscience about how he has betrayed his wife, the woman who is in agony over the impact that her work is having upon her child—all are in the middle of resolving problems that threaten their feelings of integrity and self worth. They are certainly hoping to feel good as a result.

All these people are suffering. They are all weighed down by the burden of guilt. But in every case guilt is not the end, but the means to an end.

The end? To feel good.

Feeling guilty is important precisely because it enables us to feel good for the right reasons. Like a speed limit on an open road, guilt is there to encourage a safe and a happy journey.

You may still think that guilt is designed to get you off that road to happiness, and you may still fear that saying a good word about guilt negates the possibility of feeling good. It does not, and in these next chapters I want you to see even more clearly how wrong such a conception is. To make my own conscience feel better, then, may I urge you to join me in praising that very decent and basic goal that we share?

A NEW DAWN

Feeling good. To wake up in the morning and to say: How good I feel! How I relish my life! Bring on the day!

To still feel that way at noon, and then to enjoy the rest of the working day. Not because it is free of problems, but because you know deep inside that you are strong and at peace. To lie down at night and to feel conent with what the hours before have brought.

Oh, to feel good. It seems like a dream.

Hardly anything is as greatly in demand as this emotion. No diamond is worth as much, no energy can transform as much, no song can uplift as much. Feeling good outdoes them all.

And hardly a search is pursued with as much zeal. The physical feats of the explorer who goes deep into the Amazon or the astronaut who travels deep into space cannot compare with the psychic feats of the average person who plumbs the greatest depths and scales the highest heights of his soul in search of a complex of emotions that tell him: This is paradise. Here I can be at peace.

You do not get to feel truly good by magic, though. Many paths lead to that feeling, and you must set out on them all. Feeling healthy, feeling strong, feeling happy, feeling confident —these help you to feel good. Feeling competent and feeling that you are living up to your ideals—these help, too. Feeling good comes from contentment, from a sense that you are pleased with what you have achieved. "Who is the rich man?" the Talmud asks. "He who is happy with his portion." He feels good.

BREAKING THE GUILT BARRIER

Yet, though many trails wind up this lofty peak, so many obstacles lurk on the trails to trip all those who dare to climb. Not the least of which is guilt, always there to be a stumbling block—because guilt works by inducing pain, and because you can't even imagine feeling good while you hurt.

There is, as we have seen, a purpose to this pain. But part of the problem we have in learning to live, to love, and to create with guilt is that the hurt can sometimes take on a life of its own.

Remember that in many ways guilt is like physical pain. They both have a useful purpose and they both have strange effects on people. Physical pain, we have already noted, is important for the diagnosis of disease. But different people react to pain in different ways. Some can treat mild pain by mentally blocking its effects, by "learning to live with it." Others become hypervigilant over the same pain and develop strategies for lessening it and for warding off its recurrence that become central to their lives. Often, people's reactions to pain have little connection with pain's useful purpose.

The same is even truer for guilt. It operates in the psyche to make you feel bad. And although that feeling has as its proper goal getting you to feel good, it doesn't always work that way —to say the least. Guilt comes to lead its own independent life, and the way we react to it can be far from constructive. As a result, guilt can truly become an obstacle that hinders—and even destroys—the possibility of feeling good.

The life that guilt lives on its own is marked by three features that can destroy, debilitating us instead of enabling us to feel good.

First, feeling guilty is enervating. It can undermine your "go power" and take away the running start and the motivation that each person needs to parry the slings and arrows of outrageous fortune that lie in wait twenty-four hours every day.

Second, guilt makes you punish yourself, and once the punishment begins, it may never stop.

And third, living under the weight of the self-condemnation produced by guilt, you may conclude that you are really evil at heart. The ever-present feelings of inadequacy that guilt impresses upon us have, throughout history, convinced many philosophers and laymen alike that man is essentially corrupt and that each of us is really no good at all.

Can a person seeking to feel good possibly stay on that track when faced with roadblocks like these? If not, then guilt will indeed prove to be the destructive force that many already understand it to be.

To answer this question we will have to look at each obstacle in detail, seeing what can be learned from it and how it is to be overcome. The rest of this chapter will be devoted to obstacle number one.

THE GUILT THAT TAKES YOUR BREATH AWAY

First, then, the guilt that takes your breath away, the guilt that enervates, that tires you out, that undermines your hopes.

Guilt functions like a spiritual virus. Not the kind that kills you but the kind that keeps you perennially fatigued. You keep remembering what you have done wrong and it hurts over and over again. It is simple: How can anybody be happy when there is so much about which to feel bad?

Guilt often causes some people to abandon the quest to feel good. Feeling guilty undermines their hopes and convinces them that they can never feel good. Guilt dissipates energy. By doing that it makes the goal of feeling good seem out of reach. All of us have had experiences that dash our hopes: jobs that don't work out; lovers who change their mind about loving us; illness that changes our lives. Real problems make it hard to kindle a dormant flame. Likewise, the presence of bad feelings from guilt, day in and day out, drains the energy that we need to be attached continuously to the hope that we will eventually feel good.

Guilt delivers a message that makes people feel that the search for happiness is a sham. Feeling good seems like an illusion perpetrated by those who are either too dumb or too dishonest to face the facts of life—an illusion because this thoughtful person knows that real living means feeling the pain of guilt. And once you feel guilty you can never be happy. You can never go home again.

Like Adam and Eve, many men and women know what it feels like to be banished from the Garden of Eden. Like Adam and Eve, they not only bear the psychological burden of living with the consequences of their deeds—all of us, after all, have to do that—but they see an ever-turning fiery sword that scares them away from contemplating a return to Paradise. They think that such a place is too good for them. And remembering the Bible, they feel they are in distinguished company, for has not God banished man from Paradise? Guilty man is not supposed to be happy or content. Once gone from Paradise, gone forever. Paradise is lost.

Now there is no doubt that guilt hurts and that guilt does inhibit feeling good. But does feeling guilty mean that feeling good is forever beyond our grasp? Does feeling guilty mean that you must forever feel bad?

The Bible says that God exiles Adam and Eve from Paradise and places a fearsome fiery sword to guard the way back to the Tree of Life. Note that: The way to the Tree of Life is guarded, not the way back to the Garden of Eden. God apparently doesn't want man to have eternal life. He knows, better than man, that endless time is not a gift, even if it is what man wants.

But man, even if guilty, can beat a path back to Paradise. Not to the Tree of Life, but to the lush fields that surround it. Now I admit that it is a tempting fantasy to wish that we could feel good and never feel the pangs of guilt. That is the analogue to being in Paradise *without* guilt. That option we do not, however, have. Only two choices remain. We can be guilty outside of Paradise—feeling bad without joy and hope. Or we can be guilty in Paradise—with the contentment that comes from feeling good. Shouldn't we choose to be "in" rather than "out"?

The guilt barrier can be broken. Living with guilt, we can still go back. This virus that debilitates us can be conquered. Living with guilt, we can still feel good—if we know what to do with guilt.

USE IT OR BE ABUSED BY IT

There are three responses to enervating guilt:

One . . . Be abused by it. Let its pain sap your strength. Let it take away your striving to achieve the beautiful contentment that can be achieved by human beings. Or

Two . . . Try to shoot and kill it—as though it were a ferocious bear that confronts you on the path to feeling good. But we have already seen that that is an illusion and a mistake. Or

Three . . . Use it.

Why not?

Guilt is an obstacle to feeling good, no doubt. But it is more like a boulder over which you have to climb than like a wall with no door. You pull yourself up and, lo and behold, you see that suddenly you have a new view of the terrain. The goal should not be to be abused by guilt, nor should it be to kill guilt. Rather, the only reasonable goal must be to use guilt to see where you have come from and to reroute your path.

Instead of seeing guilt as a roadblock, see it as a detour. It provides a new route. The way to battle guilt that takes away your motivation is to turn on the guilt and say: How can I use it *as* a motivation? Turn the problem on its head. Realize that guilt can be used. Then use it.

You will find that the face of guilt now takes on a new complexion. You will begin to realize that it doesn't have to sap your strength. You will derive courage from seeing this—from accepting guilt for what it is, no more and no less. But guilt will cease to be a destructive force.

Just look at how useful guilt can be.

THE USES OF GUILT

Remember, you feel guilty because. . . . You get to feel good by letting guilt be your divining rod; by finding the reason you feel guilty and by ameliorating the situation that has evolved.

If you are doing something wrong, don't do it anymore. If you have offended another person, seek to become reconciled. If you have stolen money, return the goods and pay the penalty. If you have not treated your husband, your wife, or your fourteen-year-old as you should, then do something about it. Start treating them right. Guilt is the warning signal. Now, right the wrong.

And not because there is a moralistic finger waving your way. But because you will feel good as a result. You will feel closer to the people who matter in your life. You will feel better about yourself.

Note how Gloria Norris and Joann Miller counsel working mothers. First, they say, remember rule number one: "If you really are guilty of something, stop doing it. If your child truly is suffering under your present child-care arrangement, perhaps you should consider lowering your lifestyle and paying for better care. If your child is undergoing hardships that you can trace clearly to your absence, maybe you should consider working part time." [1]

Dr. Willard Gaylin goes the same route in trying to solve a common marital problem: the fireworks that can erupt at home after a bad day at work when you were humiliated by your boss. Your husband or your wife "says something to you, and you bark at her or him, displacing the rage you did not dare show your boss. Now what happens? If you have a sense of guilt, you will feel bad and apologize. If you do not have a sense of guilt and do not apologize, then you will have converted someone who should be a comforting ally into yet another adversary." [2]

Guilt can put you back on the path to feeling good. Because guilt helps you to become aware of *what you should do*. For your own good.

The more you remind yourself of that fact, the more you realize that there is a good end to guilt, the more it will be possible for you to draw energy from your guilt instead of being demobilized by it. The more you are reminded that you can, in fact, feel good, the more it becomes plausible to you in your everyday experience that there is a nexus between the hurt you feel and the very real possibility of undoing the hurt and feeling good, the more you will triumph over guilt as a debilitating force.

GUILT IS A CATALYST

The goal, remember, is to make a connection between feeling guilty and feeling good, to perceive guilt as a positive, not a negative, force. There are many ways to accomplish this task. Try to see how it is possible to capitalize on guilt feelings. Gather the evidence and let it work on you.

Take a look at the ways in which guilt serves as a catalyst that causes useful changes to occur in others. Then you can adapt the examples to your own life. The American Red Cross, for example, has learned how to capitalize on the power of guilt. They sponsor an ad campaign designed to encourage wives to learn CPR. Then these wives will be in a position possibly to save their husbands after a heart attack. Look at the way the Red Cross cleverly uses guilt.

"What kind of wife would just stand there while her husband had a heart attack?" the ad says. "A wife who doesn't know CPR." (Turn on the guilt.) "The sad fact is, more people know how to jump-start a car than know how to save a life." (Turn it up.) "Learn Red Cross CPR." (The message delivered—or should I say clobbered home—courtesy of guilt.)

The truth is that most people don't have the time to study CPR. They are too busy with other concerns. Were you to ask them whether CPR were a good idea, they would probably say, Yes, it is a splendid idea. Someday, when I have the time, I would love to learn CPR. The problem is, then, how do you motivate people to do something which they themselves tell you they want to do?

The Red Cross is smart, and they know how people think. They know that if they can make a few wives feel guilty, a few husbands will be saved by CPR. The end result: the guilty wives will feel good. Bravo for the Red Cross and bravo for guilt!

New York Telephone has also discovered the value of guilt. They use it in an ad dubbed "The Don't Feel Guilty Call. If you don't make it, you'll be on the receiving end." In one version of this ad, a man talks to his mother on the telephone while touching a pair of bronzed baby shoes. When you look at the shoes you aren't sure whose they are, his own or those of his child, but you know the message they convey: Baby shoes make you think of your mother and how can you think of your mother without pangs of guilt? Especially if you haven't spoken with her in a while. The message concludes: "Don't feel guilty, call."

Now most men and women would agree that they want to call Mom regularly. "But," they would add, "life has become so complicated. We live so far away from one another. We work hard and are so often on the move. Of course I should keep in touch more often and I would if I could." Enter New York Telephone with the "Don't Feel Guilty Call." Mothers will be called more often because of the ad, and will consequently feel good. The children will also feel good. And it is good for New York Telephone, too. Bravo, once again, for guilt.

Don't undersell guilt. While it certainly inhibits good feelings, it is also a catalyst that enables those good feelings to grow. Guilt can be a motivational force that is hard to beat—if it is used well.

The director of an extraordinary fund-raising program explained to me that his huge success was due, in good part, to guilt. Mazon (which means "food" in Hebrew) is a fund-raising organization that asks people who are celebrating happy occasions with catered functions to donate 3 percent of the cost to Mazon. Be it a wedding, a bar mitzvah, or a birthday party, Mazon says: Take 3 percent of the cost and donate it to us.

Mazon then distributes the money collected to food programs that feed the poor. The host places cards on every festive table that is overflowing with food informing the guests that a donation has been made to Mazon so that the poor can eat. Beginning on a shoestring just a few years ago, Mazon now distributes several hundred thousand dollars a year—money that feeds the poor in communities throughout the United States.

"To what do you attribute your success?" I asked Executive Director Irving Kramer. "Guilt" was his reply. He went on to say that people who celebrate happy occasions spend a great deal of money on the food. They know quite well that while they are eating lavishly there are others who have no food at all. How do they feel? Guilty, how else? Mazon says to them, in effect, "Get rid of your guilt. Take some of your resources and give them to the poor. As you eat, let the poor eat, too."

Many people report that Mazon makes it possible for them to fully enjoy their celebrations. Otherwise they would have felt guilty about eating so much in a world where people go hungry every day.

Here, too, guilt is a catalyst that can be used for good. People have food because Mazon has capitalized on guilt. Bravo for Mazon, and bravo, once again, for guilt.

WECHSLER'S LAW OF SPECIFIC MINIMALISM

The challenge is this: Find a way to solve at least some of the problems of your life by using guilt.

Let me show you one way that I have tried, and perhaps you can apply the general principle in ways that are specifically suitable to you.

Rabbis are teachers, and our mandate is to first of all teach people the sacred texts of our faith. So years ago I began a campaign to encourage people to study the classic texts of the Jewish tradition: the Bible and the Talmud.

I found, though, that every time I mentioned study to my congregants, they told me that I was preaching to the converted for they agreed that study was a very important goal for them, too. I waited for hordes of people to come to classes. They never showed.

The problem was that no one had time. The young people said, "We are working too hard. We are working long hours so that we can become partners in our law firms, and we have young children who demand a tremendous amount of our time." So I figured that this was not the optimal age group. When I talked with people somewhat older, they explained that they were junior partners who were working to become senior partners—that their children were a little less of a burden, but that now their elderly parents were demanding a great deal of their time. And of course I knew that they were right, too. Then I spoke to those who were retired, whose children were grown, and who no longer had the burdens of work upon them. They said to me simply, "Study is the kind of activity you have to engage in when you are young."

What to do? This is a situation, I thought, that can only be solved by guilt. At first I did what comes naturally to a preacher: I exhorted the flock to study. I told them how their grandfathers and grandmothers would have given their right arms for the opportunities to learn—the books, the tapes, the videos, the beautiful classrooms that are available to us every day. In other words, I laid on the guilt.

That worked a little bit. I found that there are some people who love to feel guilty, who expect their preachers to give them a good guilt trip, and who respond beautifully. At the same time, however, I found that such an approach alienated many, particularly younger people who had had enough of guilt. In truth, though, they had had enough of the old-style guilt. What they needed was guilt served a new way.

Enter Wechsler's Law of Specific Minimalism, guilt à la nouvelle cuisine. It goes like this:

Think to yourself, "What should I be doing with my time that I know is good but that I am not doing?" Tell yourself how important it is to think about this. Say it again so that you feel really guilty. For example, "I should be reading the Bible. Here I am, forty-eight years old, and I have read books on the occult, on psychology, on computer logic, on sailing and golf, and the only thing I still know nothing about is the very civilization that Allan Bloom, in his book *The Closing of the American Mind*, tells me is the source of my own culture. I owe it to myself to study, don't I?"

Next, do not be satisfied with a generalized guilt feeling, but make it specific. For example: Decide to study the Bible and be realistic about the actual amount of time you might devote to study this year. That time is probably not very great, so don't exaggerate. Don't say you are going to read the Bible. Say, instead, that you are going to read the Book of Exodus. *Be specific.*

Be even more specific. Break Exodus up into chapters and verses. Write into your appointment book the verses you are supposed to read on Monday, Wednesday, and Friday. There is nothing like looking at your appointment book to remind you about what you are supposed to do and what, not incidentally, you were supposed to do but have not yet done. It makes you feel guilty—precisely—and that doesn't hurt one bit.

Next, the *minimalism*. After being specific, actually do less than you had planned. Why less? If you do more than you plan, you will get smug and quickly run out of steam. If you do exactly as you had intended, you may not run out of steam, but you risk losing your motivation, since study is not yet a habit ingrained for years. Instead, take advantage of guilt. If you do less, then instead of feeling smug you will feel that you are doing too little to be really satisfied with yourself. You will feel guilty, and therefore you will keep the motivational pressure on.

Now, studying the Bible may not be your highest priority. So try Wechsler's Law of Specific Minimalism with an exercise program or a series of around-the-house jobs that you have never been able to get done. Or with a task you have had difficulty completing at work. Use your inner resources to accomplish the tasks that will make you proud of your accomplishments and feeling really good about them. And remember that guilt is one of those resources that you have and can use.

Wechsler's Law of Specific Minimalism is just one example of how to tap the motivational energies found in guilt. You don't even have to drill very deep. Scratch the surface and I suspect that you will come up with some guilt that you can successfully and creatively use. Instead of working so hard, then, to get rid of guilt, hold on to some of the guilt that is naturally there and channel it in directions that enrich, rather than impoverish, your life.

That is the way to use guilt to see the terrain made up of your behavior, your feelings, your family, your job, and your aspirations. The end result of this is that you restore some of the hope that has been dissipated by feeling guilty for years. Once you realize that there is more to guilt than a feeling that hurts, you can bring yourself back to life. Get set for that trip back to Paradise. Use the guilt to help you feel good, really really good. You deserve nothing less.

CHAPTER 9
Gluttons for Punishment

The natural tendency of most people is to be swayed not by a sense of shame but by fear, and to refrain from acting basely not because it is disgraceful, but because of the punishment it brings.
—**Aristotle,** *Ethics*

There is another world for the expiation of guilt; but the wages of folly are payable here below.
—**Lord Acton**

Even God prays. What is His prayer? "May it be My will that My love of compassion overwhelm My demand for strict justice."
—**Talmud,** *Berakhot* **7a**

The first problem, then, is the enervating nature of guilt. By seeing guilt function as a positive, motivating force, and thereby reestablishing the nexus between feeling guilty and feeling good, that problem can be overcome.

The second problem brings us deeper into the painful reality of guilt, because people who feel guilty punish themselves through a familiar progression of events: You do something wrong. You know it and it hurts. Then you inflict the sentence, the punishment that the guilty party deserves. Even worse, what follows is often punishment *beyond* what is deserved, for the guilty are gluttons for punishment.

It all seems quite natural, as if everyone shares something in common with Edgar Allan Poe's guilt-ridden killer in "The Tell-Tale Heart." In this story a man commits homicide, dismembers the body and hides it in order to remove the evidence of his deed. Suddenly, there is a knock at the door: the police responding to a neighbor's report of a shriek. Confidently, the murderer conducts the police on a search. So certain is he that he has committed the perfect crime that he seats the officers in the very same room where the body rests beneath the floorboards. The officers are convinced of his innocence, but the killer begins to hear the beat of the dead man's heart. He wonders whether the police hear it as well and finally decides that they are mocking him with their feigned inattentiveness. They must know. The beating gets louder and louder.

"Villains!" the murderer finally screams, "I admit the deed!"

Poe ingeniously shows how the killer's guilt gets the best of him, forcing him to confess to the police so that he suffers the punishment he deserves for his deed. A bizarre story, no doubt, but one that is hardly unique.

Don't most people find that their guilt similarly gets the best of them? Their deeds cannot be hidden but instead beat loudly in their ears. And when they feel guilty they expect to be punished for what they have done. Not only do they expect to be punished, they go out of their way to remind their policing consciences to be attentive to their work. Outdoing "The Tell-Tale Heart," they magnify the punishments so that there will be no doubt that justice has been done.

We are no Puritans, not us. We look down on the society described in Nathaniel Hawthorne's novel *The Scarlet Letter*, a society in which Hester Prynne is punished by having to wear an "A" on her clothing to indicate her transgression. But every day many people levy far heavier punishments than the Puritans might have done—upon none other than themselves.

Mothers and fathers punish themselves for years because they know they have failed in one way or another in bringing up a child. Children suffer for a lifetime because of unresolved problems they have with their living parents and even with parents who are deceased. People get sick and fail to seek medical help, for they see their illnesses as a punishment they deserve. Others develop eating disorders, sleeping disorders, and personality disorders galore in order to punish themselves in secret ways for the unsavory deeds they have committed.

If that is the case, how can we possibly be saved from such endlessly mounting suffering, suffering which once again typifies the reckless life of guilt that has gone out on its own and that seems to know no bounds?

THE PROBLEM OF PUNISHMENT

The simplest way out of such a dilemma is to blame the idea of punishment itself and to banish it from life. But, in fact, punishment is much like guilt. Both share a bad reputation rightly deserved. And, on the other hand, each has a use which has been all but obscured by the trouble it creates.

How tempting it is to abolish punishment once and for all. To begin with, self-inflicted stripes are but one form of this degradation known all too well to the world. Generally, punishment involves the discipline of one person by another, so often with a heavy hand.

Look at the history of punishment; it is a history of cruelty. Battlefields tell its tale, battlefields strewn with corpses and battered lives that should not be there: criminals falsely accused or forced to face a firing squad for petty crimes, women beaten by their husbands, children maimed by their fathers and mothers. All in the name of doing justice and righting wrongs, of "teaching them a lesson." Battered and bloody, it is supposed, because they deserve it.

Moreover, punishment is used as a weapon not only against the body but against the mind. People feel bruised in spirit and diminished in self-esteem because they are mentally punished so much of the time.

Isaac Bashevis Singer tells the story about the time he went to the synagogue as a boy and was impressed with the shammes (sexton) who diligently did all the work in the building. If anything broke down, he took the blame. If the lights went out or the prayerbooks were torn, if it was too cold or too hot, he was blamed. "They must pay you a lot to take all this abuse," Singer said to the man. "Pay?" replied the shammes. "They pay me nothing. I do it for the honor!"

Not only that forlorn shammes, but how many others arrive at a mental state where they feel "honored" by taking the blame? Blamed for this, blamed for that, they learn that it is their lot to hurt because they deserve it.

What, then, is punishment? Usually it is cruelty delivered on the pretext that it is deserved. But it is really something more.

THE MORAL MEANING OF PUNISHMENT

Punishment has its beginnings in an intuitive sense that wrong should be properly requited. That there is and should be a connection between the way you live and the rewards you reap. Consequently, if you do evil, you should suffer evil in return. But, so often, punishment uses such an intuitive understanding as a license for cruelty. The punishment doesn't fit the crime; rather, in the words of the U. S. Constitution, it is "cruel and unusual," just as its history reveals.

Punishment, you see, is part of a larger picture, a picture that is itself necessary and useful even while subject to distortion. That picture is justice, and the scales of justice weigh out an appropriate measure of penalty for each wrong. There should no doubt be one penalty for stealing and another for kidnapping. There should be a penalty for rape and another for murder. Why the penalty? Solely to get the perpetrator off the streets? Or to "teach him a lesson he will never forget"?

There is more to punishment than that. If these were its only purposes, then other methods which might rehabilitate the criminal would recommend themselves far more. Punishment, even though it may serve the purpose of deterrence, more importantly affirms a just order, which, if undermined, weakens the whole system of morality that rests upon it.

A sensational trial recently took place in New York City which involved the death of a little girl as the result of horrendous child abuse. She was illegally adopted and repeatedly beaten by her so-called "father," until she died. Her "mother" was also brutally abused. People were outraged during the trial. They heatedly and anxiously discussed the problems of child abuse, and some have seen this as the silver lining in the upsetting public spectacle of this trial.

New York's mayor suggested that the only proper response to such outrageous behavior is to take the killer and burn him in oil for his misdeeds. When the suggestion was made, people laughed nervously. At the same time, however, they felt that it was somehow right.

At the time, I was teaching a class in social ethics to a group of graduate students, some of whom are working toward a degree in social work and do fieldwork each week in agencies throughout the city. "What is the response to this trial in your agencies?" I asked. Many people have come forward to discuss their family problems of child abuse, I was told. At the same time, however, my students made clear their fear: such a public discussion of a troubling aspect of normally private behavior runs the risk of telling people that since such practices exist, and perhaps exist widely, they are not deviant and can therefore be accepted as within the realm of acceptable behavior. The social workers' greatest fear was simply that the killer would escape punishment. For then, hundreds of thousands of people would learn that each of us can be excused for child abuse, and such terrible behavior would become sanctioned as a result.

The moral foundations of a society are held together with mortar that can be chipped away. Without the knowledge that proper punishment is the result of a crime, those moral underpinnings grow weak.

Punishment, you see, is part of the intuitive experience of justice upon which morality is based. That is why Abraham is able to confront God when he learns that the cities of Sodom and Gomorrah are doomed. What, he worries, if there are fifty righteous men? Should they be killed with all the rest? "Shall the judge of all the earth not do justly?" (Genesis 18:25). That is why the Bible presupposes a system of divine rewards and punishments. Because the God of the Bible is just, there must be a continuum of proper rewards and punishments for the actions of human beings. As in Deuteronomy, for example (11:13–14,17):

> If, then, you obey the commandments that I enjoin upon you this day, loving the Lord your God and serving Him with all your heart and soul, I will grant the rain for your land in season, the early rain and the late. You shall gather in your new grain and wine and oil. . . . Take care not to be lured away to serve other gods and bow to them. For the Lord's anger will flare up against you, and He will shut up the skies so that there will be no rain and the ground will not yield its produce; and you will soon perish from the good land that the Lord is assigning to you.

These verses from Scripture are recited by observant Jews twice each day, and constitute an individual's personal acceptance of God's commands. But they are deeply troubling to many people. They seem preposterous because they imply so primitive a relation between God and man, as if everything that happens is the product of a God who rewards and punishes human deeds.

This is not, however, what the Bible means. Not everything is the product of actions that God takes. Every time the rain falls or the sun shines, it does not mean that God is requiting evil or rewarding good. Only sometimes. The laws of nature are God's laws, and generally it is they that govern what we see here on earth. But these words of Scripture simply affirm the fact that God can, and in discrete instances, does, manifest His concern for the world by involvement in its events, and that those moments of such divine manifestations are moments that are *just*.

Indeed, it is this intuitive certainty that reward and punishment should be justly meted out that causes people to be angry when the wicked prosper and the righteous suffer. From Job until our own day, this fact has troubled the sensitive, expecting as they do that there will be a direct relationship between one's deeds and one's just deserts. Common experience is enough to teach that life doesn't work exactly that way much of the time. The book of Job reminds us that our perspectives are limited and that we do not fully understand God or His ways.

The very problem itself, however, is the best possible proof that a moral order in which there *is* reward and punishment is a reasonable expectation which can be appreciated intuitively. Otherwise we would not need theology to help us understand how it is that God can be just when the facts seem to indicate otherwise.

MORAL GEOMETRY

Reward and punishment is one way—certainly not the only one, but one way for sure—in which deeds that are moral or immoral, right or wrong, are described and reinforced in systems of justice, whether they be religious or not.

Daily living, with its many moral challenges both great and small, reminds us that there are moral equations that need to be constantly balanced each day. One of these equates doing good with the receipt of rewards, whatever they be, and doing evil with reprimands or punishments, whatever they be. Since guilt, when warranted, is understood as a judgment condemning the way we act, then it is entirely reasonable to expect punishment as a result.

In his cross-cultural study of morality and religion entitled *Religion and Moral Reason*, Professor Ronald M. Green of Dartmouth College shows that all religions, from the pagan totemism found in Africa to the religions of the Far East, from the Judaism of the Bible and the Talmud to the Christianity of Kant and Kierkegaard, accept that there is a moral continuum to which human beings must conform. They all affirm "the reality of moral retribution." [1]

The expectation of punishment is, therefore, a justified one, even if it is troubling. As a result, expecting to be punished as a result of feeling guilty should not be dismissed. Since both guilt and punishment are a necessary part of a functioning moral system, the only way to deal with them is to accept their valuable and necessary features while casting off the baggage that unnecessary guilt and excessive punishment can bring.

But beware. Remember that we are gluttons for punishment, and in practice—not in theory—punishment is normally cruel and unusual. Moreover, while punishment may be a theoretical necessity, it is really destructive and counterproductive most of the time.

Not always. In the criminal justice system, for example, its utility is sometimes compelling, as in the case of child abuse that I have described. But in dealing with your husband, your wife or your child, you are playing with dynamite. When leveled against yourself, the desire to punish is best defused.

Therefore, when you feel guilty and feel as if you should be punished, don't be surprised. Expect to feel as if punishment is called for. But don't assume that it is appropriate. It probably is not. Don't allow yourself to be taken in by what is a tempting but often destructive desire. Examine the facts, and apply some useful safety mechanisms before you handle what may be too dangerous to touch.

What are these safety mechanisms, then, that operate to make certain that punishment will be effective, appropriate and humane, and that will protect ordinary people from becoming gluttons for punishment?

First, the pain that results from the feelings of guilt must, like pretrial time spent in prison, figure into a sentence that is properly meted out. Second, make use of established rituals and customs, whether in religion or in secular culture, that effectively hold on to the reins and enable punishment to be suffered in limited and tolerable amounts. And third, balance the need for punishment with another need: the need to love and to be merciful, with others and with yourself. Religions, societies, and individuals must reckon with the fact that punishment does not stand by itself, but coexists with mercy and forgiveness. Together they transform the way we are and the way we treat our fellow human beings.

In the next chapter, let us see how these three safety mechanisms work.

CHAPTER 10

Enough Is Enough

If Thou, Lord, shouldest mark iniquities,
O Lord, who could stand?
—Psalms 130:3

It hath been told thee, O man,
what is good,
And what the Lord doth require of thee:
Only to do justly, and to love mercy,
and to walk humbly with thy God.
—Micah 6:8

Three safety mechanisms to ensure appropriate (and not unnecessary or excessive) punishment can be simply summarized: (1) feeling bad is sometimes enough; (2) constructive affliction; and (3) loving more. So often overlooked, they work hand in hand with the intuitive need for punishment and they make it possible for us to say, "Enough is enough."

FEELING BAD IS SOMETIMES ENOUGH

Sometimes, feeling guilty is punishment enough. Does a guilty person really need more? Enough is enough, and a hefty dose of guilt, well administered, can do the job. Must do the job. Because any more is nothing less than a curse.

This is the lesson that Aaron, the high priest and brother of Moses, learned, much to his surprise. It was he who felt compelled to fashion the golden calf—an idol around which the people could dance—and how do you think that Aaron, high priest of the one God who cannot be seen, felt?

Guilty, for sure, guilty as can be! After all, in the Bible, worshiping the golden calf is the archetypal sin. According to Jewish lore, the suffering of the Jewish people throughout the ages has been, in part, an effort to mete out the punishment appropriate for so horrendous a deed. Guilty, that's right.

In the Book of Leviticus, Scripture describes Moses ordering Aaron to "Come forward to the altar and sacrifice your sin offering and your burnt offering" (Leviticus 9:7). The rabbis found the authoritarian words of Moses to be out of place. Did he really have to tell Aaron to *come forward* to do his job?

A commentary explains that Aaron needed to be urged on for he was slowed down by the burden of the golden calf and the heavy weight that that memory caused him to bear on his mind. Aaron's guilt, you see, made him reluctant to come near and serve the Lord. The rabbis conclude by saying that Moses, understanding Aaron's reticence, said to him, "Come forward to the altar. Your sin has been forgiven. Because you were ashamed." [1]

Because you were ashamed. Aaron, you see, as other guilty people before and since, had paid his dues. The actual pain of the guilt was taken by the Lord to be sufficient recompense for the wrongs he had done.

Just think of what that says: When you have done wrong, you probably have an innate sense that you deserve to be punished for your wrong. You feel guilty, and you say to yourself: As a result of feeling guilty I must suffer to be sure that I have paid my dues. Beware, though. The rabbis caution you against letting guilt go to your head.

Enough is enough. Don't be a glutton for punishment. The guilt, itself the psychological punishment which you have to endure, may free you from the need for anything more.

CONSTRUCTIVE AFFLICTION

Secondly, even though it may seem rather absurd and peculiarly unmodern, spend some time thinking about useful ways to punish yourself—ways that are socially sanctioned and that may get the need out of your system before it does more harm than good. Most self-help guides to peace of mind will, I think, recommend that you abandon all such suspect desires. My perspective is different: I assume that because you are bound to feel guilty, you are bound to punish yourself. My concern is: Don't do it so that you will lose as a result. Do it so that you will win!

Since both punishment in general and self-punishment in particular make sense within the intuitive moral system shared by all guilty human beings, try to channel them into acceptable limited and tolerable forms that will defeat the temptation to act cruelly. Look to religion as a potential source for such behaviors —though there are endless possibilities.

Religions make use of *constructive afflictions*—behavior which to outsiders may seem like self-flagellation, but which to insiders is really self-protection. In Judaism, for example, Yom Kippur, the Day of Atonement, does just that.

The purpose of this day is to remind oneself of the sins committed throughout the year, sins toward God and sins toward man, so that one can repent. Now while repentance can be uplifting, recalling sins can be pretty depressing.

Some of the prayers take every single letter of the Hebrew alphabet and recite two sins that begin with each. A fascinating exercise, no doubt, but can you imagine the effect? On a normal day you may have an opportunity to reflect upon what you have done wrong, and even then it can be pretty bad. Now think about devoting a long day to nothing else, enumerating sin after sin after sin. What do you suppose that will produce?

Why, gobs and gobs of guilt, what else?

The big problem with thinking about sin is that it is depressing and dangerous. That it is depressing should be no surprise. Feeling guilty makes you feel bad. It makes you unhappy and may defuse the normal feelings of hopefulness with which you live. What stinging questions are asked: Why am I not a better person? Why does it seem that this year I am not much better than I was a year ago?

Depressed, depressed, depressed.

And dangerous, too. Because it is a wholly natural reaction to imbibe the guilt and to expect to be punished for the wrongs you have done. And the more the merrier, or should I say, the more you sin, the worse you feel.

What is the temptation, then? To punish yourself and to punish yourself really well. To go at it in a big way: to afflict yourself with horrible afflictions. Know that you are a worm and treat yourself that way. Change your eating patterns and eat only those things that taste terrible. Or, even better, don't eat anything at all—starve yourself to make yourself really pay. Afflict your body. Be dirty. Go around barefoot. Sex? Forget it. Anything that smacks of pleasure is not for you.

Take it from there. What I am simply trying to say to you is that the temptation for affliction is immense. So immense, in fact, that it is possible that life will turn into an affliction all because of guilt.

How to be saved? *Constructive affliction.* On the Day of Atonement, Scripture says to "afflict your souls" (Numbers 29:7). On that day a Jew is forbidden to eat, to drink, to wash (beyond the minimal necessities of hygiene), to enjoy the normal comforts of rubbing one's skin with oils or wearing leather shoes, even to have sexual relations with one's spouse.

The Day of Atonement comes one day a year. Just one day. It is as if we are saying: Go ahead, afflict yourself, hurt yourself, go to it. But follow the rules so you don't get carried away. And only for one day, please. More than that, you have a problem, not a prescription for healthy living. And such problems healthy people don't need.

Self-punishment is a thoroughly natural part of a person's life —which is not to say, though, that it should be inflicted without end. Enough is enough.

What options do you have? Yom Kippur? Lent? Ramadan? Weight-Watchers? Feeling the pain of running three miles each day? Going backpacking for two weeks? Wearing torn and dirty jeans? Realize that in every religion and in all cultures there are ways to allow self-affliction, and to mediate its harmful side-effects. Look around and see what options are yours.

MORE CONSTRUCTIVE AFFLICTIONS

A similar experience in self-affliction is the lot of the bereaved. A person who has lost a loved one is oftentimes filled with a sense of grief that contains a large component of guilt. I refer not to some of the more profound sides of melancholy that are the province of the psychiatrist, but to the more common feeling most mourners have. The feeling, for example, that there is unfinished business that was not resolved.

As hard as it normally is to face a loved one's death, there are situations where mourners have had no opportunity to iron out the wrinkles in their relationships with the deceased. And when death comes, there is no more time.

But the extreme case hides a common experience which most of us have: that after a loved one has died we will never again have the opportunity to do what we were waiting for special circumstances to do. I remember driving to the cemetery in a limousine once with a woman who kept repeating again and again, "Why didn't I have the painters come six months ago?" She could no longer invite the deceased to the dinner party she had put off. Another time, I remember a man standing at the graveside of his wife. He shed tears as he said to her, "I never told you this before, but I loved you so much." Why, I thought, have you waited until now?

In different ways, though, every one of us has unfinished business with the ones we love. Every one of us has missed opportunities to be good, to forgive, to laugh, to embrace those who are now gone.

When they are dead, so many people suddenly become alive —alive in the sense that their presence is finally appreciated. Scholars and authors finally achieve their deserved fame—posthumously. Business partners and husbands and wives finally are appreciated—posthumously.

My teacher, the late Rabbi Max Arzt, used to tell the story of a woman who ran up to him after he had delivered a speech. "Rabbi Arzt," she said, "I so much look forward to reading your words posthumously." She would not be the first person to confront a rabbi, a cantor, a minister, a professor, or a politician with that sorry reminder of what it often takes to be appreciated.

And this phenomenon is neither unique nor the result of the moral laxity of a few scattered human beings. Rather, Rabbi Joseph B. Soloveitchik correctly notes, human beings are forever guilty because their "appreciation of persons, things, and events is always a product of hindsight."[2] Only when someone is no longer here do we really feel, most cogently, how special and unique that person was. And how does that make us feel? Guilty, of course.

There is no more difficult situation than one which is unpleasant and which you cannot change. And here you are feeling guilty, when there is nothing further you can do to assuage the guilt. If you have wronged a person during his or her lifetime there is always the alternative of asking for forgiveness and turning from one's ways. That is no longer possible once death has intervened. And there is no way that we can save ourselves from the natural guilt that mourning brings.

The problem is that we will persecute and punish ourselves ad nauseam for this guilt that cannot be assuaged. There are, in fact, cultures where people cut their flesh when a loved one has died. They punish themselves severely for the guilt that they feel.

But it is precisely because of this that Judaism prescribes a mourning period that lasts seven days in its most intense phase. During that time, one afflicts one's body in ways that are remarkably like some of the afflictions of Yom Kippur, minus the prohibition against eating and drinking. Aspects of this affliction go on for a month. After the death of a mother or a father, some afflictions continue for a year.

People often look at those who observe these mourning customs and wonder why it is that such people want to make their lives miserable. The truth is that the mourning customs are not the source of their misery. Their sadness comes from the fact that they are bereaved. Mourning provides *constructive afflictions*, structured forms for people to respond to the normal feelings of guilt that they have and to afflict themselves within very prescribed boundaries. Otherwise, you just don't know how the intense feelings of guilt will manifest themselves, nor what afflictions people will choose.

Guilt is a natural part of the response to the experience of death. It generates the need for self-punishment. But once again, enough is enough. It is proper and reasonable to engage in the guilt that comes when a loved one is gone. But it is important to know that a certain amount of suffering is appropriate to expiate a wrong. It is not a sign of weakness if you feel guilt at a loved one's death, as long as the suffering brought about by guilt can come to an end, and life can go on.

Do not expect the death of a loved one to pass by easily. There are bound to be unresolved problems, guilt that will lead to self-punishment. Be careful, though, once again to ask: What are your options? There is nothing wrong with wanting to experience hurt. It may be the best thing, as long as you don't want it too much.

Jews have a custom of giving charity in memory of the deceased. I often recommend to people that they give until it hurts. Strangely, by so doing they help not only the poor but themselves as well.

The problem of punishment is, then, a problem that comes along with guilt. As with guilt, it has its purposes, purposes that are part of the intuitive way that morality works. But as with guilt, it has its problems, too. Punishment tends to be cruel. Whether used on others or used on oneself, it is more often cruel than not. The second need, then, as we have just seen, is to find ways to allow that need to be expressed while making certain that cruelty does not reign.

But still, punishment can be dangerous.

LOVING MORE

There is a third necessary antidote to the problems of punishment—the antidote of love. Professor Green, in his study of morals and religion, makes the point that religions possess "beliefs that suspend moral judgment and retribution when this is needed to overcome moral paralysis and despair . . . in response to the kind of self-condemnation that inevitably accompanies sensitive moral striving, they are prepared to ease their insistence on judgment and retribution by holding out the promise of a redemption not based entirely on one's deeds."[3]

That redemption, in fact, is based on mercy and love. When God weighs the deeds of human beings and finds them wanting, what is the human response? To ask God for mercy. To appeal to His love. When human beings treat each other with exacting justice and seek to requite wrongs that are done, what appeal can we make to each other? The appeal for love.

The story is told of the Baal Shem Tov, the founder of Hasidism, who served as a religious and psychological counselor to his pious adherents. One day a man came to see him because he was having great difficulty with his child. The boy had committed many, many wrongs. And the father came to the rabbi to find out what he should do. He put his case before the Baal Shem Tov, showing the rabbi that he had been careful not to spare the rod, lest his master think that the boy was a spoiled child.

The Baal Shem Tov listened to the father's plea for advice and finally told him simply, "Try loving him more."

This, you see, is the true antidote for punishment: love. This is the ingredient that must go together with retribution in creating a moral system that is both effective and humane. This is the balance that must be kept, the balance between justice and love.

God created the world, mixing justice and mercy together, say the rabbis. To what can this process be compared? To a king who had two fine crystal cups. Said the king: "If I fill them with hot water, then they will expand and break. If I fill them with cold water, they will contract and shatter." What did the king do? He mixed the hot and the cold together, poured them in, and the cups were just fine.

So said the Holy One Blessed Be He, the rabbis continue: "If I create the world with only mercy in it, sins will multiply. If only with justice, then how can it stand? Rather I shall create it with justice and with mercy. Let it then go on!"[4]

Punishment grows out of a sense of justice. What justice needs, for balance, is love.

That is ultimately the purpose of the Day of Atonement: to appeal to God as a loving God, and to know that God's love can mitigate all wrongs. And that is the purpose of loving one another. Not to substitute feelings of love for the need to maintain a system of justice. But to be sure that justice will be pursued humanely and divinely; that justice will be meted out, safe from cruelty; that it will be accompanied by love.

Love and mercy therefore constitute the final means of protection against the dangers of punishment. We need to love others to be sure that we will not punish them too much. We need to love ourselves in order to make sure that we will not punish ourselves too much. We need to cultivate the emotion of love as much as we need to strive for justice and reach for morality.

Do not deny the need for punishment. But try to reduce it to an absolute minimum, using certain forms of behavior that are not destructive, and developing the power of love that is expressed personally and toward others so that punishment, though an important theoretical reality, will be an unimportant practical one.

The purpose of guilt, remember, is to make us feel good for the right reasons. It raises moral issues, and all the parameters of the moral equation, including the need for retribution, will be raised as well. Living with guilt requires the resolution of what seem like side issues such as punishment to make certain that we will still feel good in the end.

CHAPTER 11

Being Guilty

Surely, if you do right, there is uplift.
But if you do not do right, sin couches at
the door; its urge is toward you, yet you
can be its master.
—Genesis 4:7

For there is no distinction; since all have
sinned and fall short of the glory of God,
they are justified by His grace as a gift,
through the redemption which is in
Christ Jesus, whom God put forward as
an expiation by His blood, to be received
by faith.
—St. Paul, *Letter to the Romans* 3:22

Feeling good yet? Would that it were so simple!

There are, you remember, three ways that guilt hinders—and even destroys—the possibility of feeling good. First, in Chapter 8, we looked at the enervating nature of guilt. Then, in Chapters 9 and 10, we looked at the tendency of guilt to make you punish yourself. The third hindrance still remains: that guilt will convince you that you are really evil at heart.

GUILT: CAN'T LIVE WITH IT!

If only guilt were a help. If *feeling guilty* were only a barometer of a troubled soul and if, reading the barometer, the soul would benefit from the messages that it receives. If a *guilty conscience* were only a guide for the moral tasks of the intellect and if each person would benefit from the control that the intellect could exert.

More often, though, guilt makes a person feel like a nuclear reactor well on its way to meltdown. It is less often the longed-for cure for a dread disease than the Chernobyl of the soul.

To suggest using the emotions and the intellect for such a lofty purpose may make a guilt trip sound like a vacation rather than the prison it really is.

The truth is that while guilt may be a cure for spiritual ill-nesses, the cure is often worse than the disease! Worse not only because of the pain suffered. That would be unpleasant, but tolerable, were it certain that the pain was all for a good cause. But is it?

Guilt lights a fire that burns our castles down. Instead of teaching us something that will be spiritually uplifting—even if only in the long run—it just as often (perhaps even more often) delivers a message that is perhaps the most deeply disabling message of all. For guilt teaches us—erroneously—that not only have we done wrong, but worse: *that we are bad.*

Take a common situation: A child grows up from infancy with parents who sow guilt with hundreds of seeds. Their intentions are noble and they are being good parents by teaching their child the difference between right and wrong. I am their biggest supporter and God help the child who doesn't have parents like that.

The pedagogy begins with a hefty dose of "thou shalt nots" —as it should. It goes on and on, providing a clear sense of what the right path is on which this child should walk. But what happens when a line is passed, when a child begins to hear not only the message that hitting someone is bad, or acting boisterously is not proper, but also begins to hear, "I am bad." As he grows up, he says to himself, "I am criticized so much. I feel guilty toward my parents. I feel guilty toward God. I must be a terrible person." That is the beginning of meltdown.

Or take the troublesome issue of sex and sexuality, so widely discussed in recent years. The moral traditions of nearly all religions forbid a whole variety of sexual behaviors. That is certainly true in Judaism, where the prohibition against adultery is one of the Ten Commandments and where additional prohibitions go far beyond that.

Traditional faiths generally teach modesty and the importance of channeling natural urges into the lasting mutual relation of marriage. But a lot of other messages are, no doubt, conveyed along the way. It is very easy to hear the message: You shall have no relations with a partner other than your spouse. But it is, alas, also very easy to infer from it: There is something wrong with the *feelings* I long to express. My conscience seems to be teaching me that my natural longings are wrong. There is something *bad* about my body which is the cause of so many critical rules. The whole subject is conceived of as "dirty."

The line is swiftly passed from confronting a moral standard to learning that the person with the desires and with the forbidden urges, the person who often fails—*that person is bad.* Feeling guilty and having a guilty conscience turn into "being guilty."

Two messages are conveyed by guilt. At first: *What I am doing* is wrong. But then comes a second: *I must be pretty bad* to do such awful things. Time goes on and the two messages meld into one, guilt taking the rap: *I am guilty.* The verdict is in.

Not that I feel guilty and learn from my feelings how to repair my life. Not that my conscience is stirred to make me a better person. But I *am* guilty. The verdict is in on my life and it is not good. I am repulsed by myself. Every fiber of my being seems to cough from the pollution of my creation. I am guilty to the core.

ONTOLOGICAL GUILT

Guilt comes to have another meaning. It is not a verdict leveled against actions but a verdict on life. And not only my life.

Experience teaches that other people are not much better. We generalize: People are pretty bad, and that is just the way it is. Not liking such an assessment of the human condition, we blame it on God: God creates man guilty. Guilt, as philosophers say, is an ontological fact of life.

Ontological: That is to say, guilt is no longer contingent upon any changing circumstance. Not: I am guilty because . . . But simply: I am guilty. God created me guilty. Guilty have I come forth from my mother's womb. Guilt is written into the DNA of my being.

What began as a psychological state, a feeling *(feeling guilty)* or an idea *(having a guilty conscience)*, has turned into an *ontological* state: I *am* guilty. And it is here that the true trouble begins.

The problem is simply this: While feeling guilty and having a guilty conscience make good sense, they often teach a lesson that they need not teach. They convey the message that my *being* is guilty and that *I am bad*. Guilt is no longer an exit point from human folly, the feeling that turns you around to go from darkness to light; guilt weaves its own web, as complex as that woven by any spider. It ensnares the free-flying spirit and snuffs out its life.

That is just what Joseph K. learns in Franz Kafka's novel *The Trial*. He starts off happy and discovers that he is being choked by incomprehensible guilt. Joseph K. is arrested by officials. He expects an explanation of the charges against him, confident that he has done nothing wrong. But when he gets to court he finds that all cases are forgone conclusions, that no one has ever been acquitted, and that the court operates in complete secrecy. K. is condemned by a law he does not understand and which is inscrutable when approached. He understands nothing about his guilt save the fact of the guilt itself.

So much then for praise of the law: "The law of the Lord is perfect, restoring the soul" (Psalm 19:8). Kafka articulates the more common perception that the laws and rules that govern human life have a sinister side to them. Rather than liberate the spirit, they incarcerate it. At every turn there is a sense of guilt, and at some point the reasons for being guilty are no longer evident. The inscrutable sense of suffering from guilt comes to dominate a person's life. Guilt moves from being a state of mind to a primary part of the state of being human.

Isn't that one of the main reasons why the subject of guilt troubles so many people, why guilt is perceived as a terrible evil to be destroyed by any and all means? Because guilt seems to get you nowhere. It leads down blind alleys. It distorts all the good things we think about ourselves and the happy thoughts we harbor about our futures. As the Yiddish proverb has it: With friends like that, who needs enemies?

TWO KINDS OF GUILT, TWO VIEWS OF EVIL

As we have now seen, there are really two kinds of guilt: *ontological guilt* and *psychological guilt.* One of the reasons we have so much difficulty handling guilt is simply that these two kinds of guilt normally go by the same name. Being guilty is being guilty, right? But they are not the same.

They may begin similarly. Guilt breeds dread, fear, and terror. But when it goes on to breed the compelling and troubling certainty that human existence is built on an evil foundation, that we are bad, then it becomes ontological guilt. Ontological guilt arises where evil itself is understood to be a part of the essential fabric of being.

Not so for *psychological* guilt. In psychological guilt, guilt is a feeling or a state of mind that results from error or wrongdoing. You feel bad because you have done something wrong. Because you have done wicked things, your barometer registers the deviation from the norm. Feelings send messages to the conscience, and conscience transforms this unbalanced state of affairs into an action plan that can restore the soul's equilibrium.

With *ontological* guilt, on the other hand, when a person is filled with the dread it causes, he wants to direct his heaviest ammunition against it. Being guilty begs for a radical change because being guilty oppresses a person endlessly. Since ontological guilt is a building block in the foundation of human creation, it is hard to extricate. Like the strange Biblical house that is found to have leprosy, it must be completely destroyed (Leviticus 14:43–45).

PRIMORDIAL EVIL

Ontological guilt has its roots deep in pagan religion. It can be seen in religious systems where evil is considered so much a part of the universe that it is thought to predate the creation of man. Fate, for example, which wreaks havoc on Greek heroes who assume they are above its powerful grasp, affects the gods as well. In mythological systems there are good gods and there are bad gods. And, particularly in the ancient Mesopotamian world, the gods were thought to be capricious, impulsively creating the varied woes and troubles that befall human life.

Ancient man looked to magic because he was nervous, because he felt the tremendous power of evil in the universe impinging upon him with every step he took. Like a child who is afraid to step on the cracks when he walks on the sidewalk lest his luck turn bad, a pagan was similarly anxious about every move he made. Evil was so much a part of the reckless behavior of the gods that anxiety was the result for human beings. You had to be afraid of everything you did and every place you walked, for who knew? The power of evil might come to strike you down.

And it very well might be that you were being punished for your sins—that the gods had a hidden agenda after all. If this were the case, evil would stalk you with even more intensity. Guilt—terrible guilt—was the result.

Early on in civilization, pagans conceived of the possibility of expiating sin. They developed the idea that a sacrifice might get rid of a god's wrath. And, since evil had such a powerful source, the removal of its troubling hand required a powerful gift to the gods. Among the ancient Greeks and the Romans, for example, a human being would be sacrificed to stop the power of evil from having its effect. It was a drastic form of atonement.

Among the Greeks there were rites associated with what they called the *pharmakos*. The *pharmakos* was the peculiarly Greek form of scapegoat. In Archaic times, each year a man would be driven out of the city, or even killed, in accordance with a fixed rite of humiliation to secure purification for the country that year.

During the Feast of Thargalia in Athens, a feast dedicated to the god Apollo, a man and a woman would be stoned or driven out of the city—one for all the men of Athens, and one for all the women. Often the *pharmakos* was a person who deserved punishment, and therefore on the Island of Leucas a criminal was thrown into the sea every year in a sacrifice to Apollo in order to ward off evil.[1] Notice this now: a yearly ritual of atonement involving human sacrifices designed to propitiate the gods.

The pagans had consciences. But they lived in a world where evil was ontological in origin. With a large gesture, with human sacrifice, evil, too, could be warded off and misdeeds atoned for.

The method of atonement is crucial here: it is heavy-artillery atonement, sacrificing human life. It gives a clue to the deep-rootedness of the guilt it tries to assuage. Of a lesser degree, but similarly, think of the story of Oedipus the King. He has sinned unwittingly by sleeping with his mother, but even such unintentional sins were the possible cause of terrible divine wrath. The stakes are very high, and what does he do to atone? He plucks out his eyes.

The stakes are so high, the power of evil so great, the rootedness of the guilt so deep, that extraordinary deeds alone can compensate for its overwhelming power.

THE LIBERATING POWER OF CHRISTIANITY

But man needs to be liberated from such horrendous evil. It is in light of such a background that one can understand the great power of Christianity to transform ancient man and to bring him into the universe of discourse that is found in the Bible.

Think: If evil were so terrible and the need for atonement so great, and if there were an effective way of ridding those forces of evil of their power by vicariously sacrificing a person as was commonly done in the Greek world, how much more effective would it be if one person might die for all people. More extraordinary and more effective yet, if that person were also a god who died for humanity. To rid humanity of its sinfulness and to then allow mankind to be saved and able to rid itself of this primordial guilt—this would be the ultimate means to transform the ontological idea of evil into a manageable and less virulent ill.

With brilliance, then, Christianity transformed the culture of ancient man so afflicted with ontological evil and ontological guilt. In a world that began with such pagan conceptions, the way to liberate man was to conceive of his sin as atoned by the most powerful means of all: the sacrifice of a man who was God.

EVIL CREATED BY MAN

But what of *psychological guilt?* How does it differ from ontological guilt?

First of all, its starting point is entirely different. Man is not evil. Neither is God. Man creates evil by his deeds. The great Bible scholar and theologian Yehezkel Kaufmann wrote in his monumental study *The Religion of Israel* that in the Bible "Evil has no special divine preexistence. Evil comes into the world on account of sin."[2]

First of all, then, Kaufmann makes it clear that the Bible denies the power of evil over God. Secondly, we do not sin because God created us with evil centers. According to Scripture, after God creates the world complete with man, He looks at it and says: It is *very* good. Before man was created God looked and evaluated the situation several times saying that it was good. But the phrase "very good" appears only after the creation of man.

Man is not evil. He is created by God and God says that man is part of what is very good.

Then why is the world such a bad place? What went wrong? Who went wrong?

You went wrong and I went wrong. God created us with great *potential.* We *could be* very good. But are we all that we might be? We do wrongly. We abandon the right path. We wander and we stray. Because we are free to do so and because we also harbor desires that lead us astray.

God, you see, gave Adam a few commandments, some basic rules by which to live. And He also gave Adam the free will to choose whether to live by these rules or not. Right from the start, when Adam is told what he should do, he thinks it over and he says to himself, "Well, maybe I should do something else."

That is how evil enters the world. For *psychological* reasons. Because of human motivations. Because of feelings. Because of lack of control. Sin is essentially a psychological state of wrongdoing as seen with Biblical eyes. Evil is man-made, not God-made, and the way to get rid of it is through the appropriation of all those factors that affect human behavior, those factors that are emotional as well as rational, in order to change our deeds.

Guilt is part of the system for change. From this perspective it is wrongly viewed as ontological. Its dread is not essential but temporary, coming and going as the need arises. It is a psychological state which is part of the yearning to reach higher and to perfect the imperfect state of human life.

Imperfection is ontological. Guilt is not.

Let us see what it means to live with such imperfection, for this is really our problem and this is the proper area for guilt to affect our lives.

PART IV
Getting Rid of Guilt by Properly Channeling It

CHAPTER 12
The Paradox of Perfection

As for God, His way is perfect . . .
—Psalms 18:31

*In small proportions we just
beauties see,
And in short measures life may
perfect be.*
—Ben Jonson

*Charity, dear Miss Prism, charity! None
of us are perfect. I myself am peculiarly
susceptible to draughts.*
—Oscar Wilde,
The Importance of Being Earnest

Attached to all human aspirations is the paradox of perfection: the reality that perfection is conceivable but rarely attainable. And even when attainable, it is impossible to sustain for very long.

On the one hand, each of us has a vision, sometimes vague and sometimes clear, of what should be. A vision of the physical world, for example, which approaches perfect beauty. A philosophical vision of a pure and perfect idea and a certainty of its truth. A moral vision of a virtuous life, replete with good deeds. These are just a few of the extraordinary landscapes that the mind's eye can see and that can be such a source of energy and uplift.

And yet, time after time, clouds roll in. Sometimes we are disappointed that we cannot achieve the perfection we want. Other times the very notion of perfection changes right before our eyes. The perfect painting we loved yesterday looks less beautiful today, and that perfect picture is yet to be painted. What is valued as beauty by one generation is deemed ostentation by the next. The philosopher's truth is seen to be only a partial truth at best. The virtuous person is revealed to be corrupt. In ever so many ways, we fail to be what we are in our dreams, and that failure serves as a reminder that we are imperfect. A reminder that hurts.

BECAUSE YOU ARE IMPERFECT, YOU FEEL GUILTY

Imperfection. You love your husband, but it is an *imperfect* love. He isn't compassionate or concerned with the details of your life. He is sometimes cruel and often controlling. There is anger in your love.

You love your mother, but that too is an *imperfect* love. She smothers you with affection and treats you as if you will never grow up. She makes you feel that whatever you do for her is not enough. Not only is there anger, but there are doubts in your love. You love her, yes, but with an ambivalent love.

You love your child, and yet even that is an *imperfect* love, a love that keeps a log of frustrations and disappointments. Some of its pages describe the endless self-centeredness of a growing child, the arrogance of a two-year-old or a teenager, and others tell of the ways that children act out their anger when choosing their spouses or moving to the other side of the world.

You love an imperfect love and you feel guilty for every conflicting feeling that coexists with your love.

Imperfection. You are committed to your career and you do your best to excel in your work. But you perform *imperfectly.* There is always a typo you miss, a deadline you forget. Your own report card, let alone your superior's evaluation, gives you plenty of reason to be disappointed in yourself. You feel guilty that you don't do a better job.

Now these are not the guilt pangs that come from having done egregious wrongs, not the results of committing murder or theft. They are the annoying bad feelings with which a person lives every day, the petty verdicts that come in so often and that tarnish a person's image of himself.

We feel guilty *because we are terribly aware of how imperfect we are.*

GUILT AND SHAME

This is an inevitable guilt, and it is inextricably mixed with shame. Moral philosophers and psychologists commonly speak of the distinction between guilt and shame. Sometimes, it is a distinction that is forced and the two words are used to mean the same thing. But often, guilt and shame have been distinguished on the basis of whether there are internal or external sanctions that cause this emotional state to be produced. Guilt has traditionally been understood to imply feelings that are self-produced; shame, to imply feelings that are produced by others.

Recent moral philosophy, however, has introduced another, more useful, distinction. Here, guilt is understood to be the result of transgressing boundaries, of breaking the rules we have come to accept. Shame, on the other hand, is produced as a result of failing to realize one's aspirations.[1] As John Rawls explains, "One may be ashamed of his appearance or slow-wittedness. Normally these attributes are not voluntary and so they do not render us blameworthy; yet given the tie between shame and self-respect, the reason for being downcast by them is straightforward."[2]

The two are, however, inextricably linked, because they both come from an awareness of our essential imperfection, a state that can never be completely overcome. Guilt is, strictly speaking, how you feel when you have *done* wrong. Shame is how you feel when you know you fall short of your own ideals. In reality, shame and guilt coexist much of the time.

For example, I remember a man who felt guilty for having lung cancer and who was ashamed at the same time. What do you mean? I asked. He had been a smoker and I assumed that he felt guilty for having caused his disease. But that was not the reason. Years ago he had quit smoking, and was fully convinced that since he could not have known what was harmful about having been a smoker (medical researchers in those days not having yet discovered the link between smoking and lung cancer), he had no reason to be guilty. He explained, instead, that he was sure that he still heard his mother saying, when he came home with a cold, "Why didn't you wear your rubbers?" He heard his mother again now. He felt, therefore, a very primitive and really inappropriate guilt. As I probed further it became clear that there was another level—he was ashamed to be so vulnerable. He had been a runner, an athlete, the picture of perfect health, and alas, he fit that picture no more.

We act imperfectly and are guilty as a result. We have a self-image that exceeds our reach and we are ashamed.

TIME HIGHLIGHTS IMPERFECTION

The incorrigible, ever moving reality of time only heightens the sense of imperfection and increases the guilt and the shame.

Let us say that you struggle to balance your family, your work, and your own personal needs every single day. You struggle to find the time to serve them all equally well. Yet the cards are stacked against you because there is never enough time to go around.

There is inevitably too little time for having those important conversations with your husband or your wife. There is too little time for reading a story with Junior tonight before bed. There is too little time to call your parents or your sisters and brothers, let alone to go to the doctor when you yourself are not feeling well. And *you feel guilty* in return. Guilty for what you don't do. Ashamed of how you have failed.

Time won't stand still long enough for us to perfect our lives. We can never have enough time. Large numbers of families I know have bought personal computers with the hope of saving time and bringing order back into their chaotic lives—order that will save them from guilt. The memory skills of these computers have been growing every year. They started out at 64K and they are now moving up to a megabyte or more, as one says in computerese. With a million things to do every day, you need a million bits of information in your computer to even hope to begin to triumph over the feeling that it will always be impossible to keep up with your responsibilities to others—and to yourself.

A woman confided to me some while ago that computer technology has still not solved her problem. She can't use her computer because she has no time to learn how it works. And she now feels guilty and ashamed because she has failed once again to bring order into her all too imperfect life.

But more difficult yet is the realization that as much as we can never *have* enough time or money to achieve perfect lives, we can also never *be* enough to be satisfied with ourselves. Actions, too, are inevitably suffused with frustration and imperfection. The better you are, the more you become aware of how much better you could be. And, if anything, religions simply heighten this sensitivity because they provide long lists of goals for individuals to achieve.

My teacher, the late Professor Abraham Joshua Heschel, enjoyed impressing his students with this fact. Several years ago he delivered a series of lectures at the University of California that were later published as his book *Who Is Man?* When he was lecturing on the relation between religion and ethics, a professor asked him the "sixty-four-thousand dollar" question. "Why," he asked, "do I need religion? I am a good person. I treat others decently. I lead an honest and an ethical life. What does religion have to offer me?"

To which Professor Heschel answered, "That is the difference between you and me. You are a good person. I am not." And at this point Professor Heschel went on to explain that an observant Jew recites a prayer three times a day in which he says to God, "Forgive us, for we have sinned." Religion, you see, heightens man's awareness of his moral imperfection. But not, as you might think, in order to undermine his life.

Religion provides the impetus to allow us to touch the stars. Yet knowing that we could be better is a mixed blessing that produces a great deal of guilt and shame. There is no way to avoid it. The human condition is such that we are blessed by being able to have visions. We are blessed by the power to dream. But King Midas we are not; the gold we touch inevitably turns to dust.

SOMEBODY OUT THERE MUST BE PERFECT

Or does it? The Greeks believed in the possibility of perfection. Look at their statues, which represent physical perfection. That perfection was actively pursued and the pursuers were pleased with what they achieved. Kenneth Clark, in his classic study *The Nude*, cites the words of Kritobalos in the *Symposium* of Xenophon as illustrative of a general attitude: "What do I care for any man? I am beautiful."[3]

Arrogance, yes. But Clark contends that this is merely one aspect of a pride and confidence in the body seen especially in the tradition of young men who display themselves naked on the sports field. Clark notes: "Greek confidence in the body can be understood only in relation to their philosophy. It expresses above all their sense of human wholeness."[4] And, I might add, the certainty that such wholeness was within common reach, the certainty that perfection could be achieved. Contrast this, for a moment, with the Biblical perspective on the human body: to have God cover it as a sign of the embarrassment felt by a vulnerable human being.

To the Greeks, moral perfection was likewise an achievable virtue. Aristotle, for example, felt that it is characteristic of good men that they do no wrong.[5] He who is most virtuous has not stumbled before and the penitent is, consequently, a bad man. Compare this with the Biblical belief that "there is not a righteous man upon earth, that doeth good, and sinneth not" (Ecclesiastes 7:20, 1 Kings 8:46, 2 Chronicles 6:36).[6] The Bible emphasizes the need for man to turn from his evil ways, as Isaiah put it: "Let the wicked forsake his way, and the man of iniquity his thoughts: and let him return unto the Lord, and He will have compassion upon him, and to our God, for He will abundantly pardon" (Isaiah 55:7).[7]

That is not to say that the human body as pictured by the Greeks is not beautiful, and that an effort to achieve physical perfection is evil. It is also not to say that a lofty notion of virtue, Aristotle's or someone else's, is a corrupt idea. All of these pictures of perfection are useful and worthwhile as long as they are recognized as aspirations that, even if reached, are ephemeral.

For even the greatest physical beauty decays. Even if Oscar Wilde's Dorian Gray would not age and could miraculously hold on to his physical beauty, his picture decayed. And ultimately, of course, he could not stand to see that beauty must inevitably pass away.[8]

And even the greatest and most important human beings sin. When the book of Leviticus lists those who are required to bring a sin offering, it begins with the "anointed priest" (Leviticus 4:3). Even he who is the most important religious leader of his day is not infallible. And his sin offering, therefore, must come first.

Immediately after the high priest, the Sanhedrin,[9] or supreme court, brings the next offering. Its leadership embodies the highest judicial and moral ideals of the nation, and its members are looked up to for guidance. But even the members of the court can sin, and they must acknowledge their guilt and bring a sin offering.

Next is the head of state (Leviticus 4:22). He too does wrong, and he, too, needs to bring a sin offering.[10] Finally, "If any one of the common people sin through error . . ." (4:27). But, of course, we know that common people sin.

There is no way to do away with the problem of imperfection. The greatest are imperfect. The less great are imperfect. The High Priest and the common man are imperfect. Such is the state of human moral affairs.

You would like to be different? Then you would be an angel and not a human being. And since there is no way to abolish imperfection, there is no way to abolish guilt. There is only a need to ask: What can imperfect creatures do?

A great deal!

TO BE A HOLY ARK

According to the Torah, when the Ark was built to house the holy tablets of the law, its dimensions were decreed by Scripture to be two and a half cubits in length, one and a half cubits in width, and another cubit and a half in height (Exodus 25:10). A fourteenth-century Spanish rabbi, Jacob ben Asher, noticed how unusual it was for Scripture to describe the Ark's dimensions in halves: two *and a half*, by one *and a half*. You might have thought, he says, that this would be a *perfect* Ark, all its dimensions complete: two by one or three by two. The point of Scripture is, however, that an imperfect Ark *does* contain the Tablets of the Law. Because *imperfect vessels can contain holiness:* That is what Scripture wants us to learn.

But who learns it? We become so easily tempted by all that we can know and all that we can become that we think we can and must be perfect.

Young couples contemplating marriage expect to have perfect marriages. They have learned that there is a key to that perfection, and it is love. But the assumption is, then, that if you love someone you will have bliss, and if you don't have unending happiness, it must mean that you don't love your spouse and you must have made the wrong choice. Somebody is bad, unfit for marriage, and therefore it won't work.

We expect perfection and assume that anything less reveals a fatal flaw. We immediately fall back on the idea that evil is a building block and that we must uproot it totally in order to make things good. Again, what we should expect is imperfection. What we should try to do is create holiness that will reside in an imperfect ark. Marriage provides that ark so that two people can create holiness in it together.

People today seek to perform perfectly in both their careers and in their roles as parents. As our reward, we expect perfect jobs and perfect kids. If we receive anything less we assume we must have a fatal flaw. Then we feel guilty that we are so flawed. It seems like the curse of our creation, and as if we can succeed only through some sort of radical change.

Rather, we should expect imperfection. Then, when we feel guilty, we will not become depressed at the unchangeable flaws with which we have been created. Rather, guilt will reveal a specific and probably changeable circumstance that can make our lives, our jobs, and our children better for us.

Strange though it may seem, imperfect creatures are exactly the creatures that God wanted to create in this world. A Roman general is said to have asked Rabbi Akiba why God did not create man already circumcised. The Roman knew that it was Jewish practice to circumcise male children on the eighth day of life, and to him the practice seemed absurd. Jews, he reasoned, believe that man is created in the image of God. God is perfect, and, it would stand to reason, has created a world that does not need any human tampering. How could Jews then believe that we human beings have the right to change the physical creation of man, especially by removing a part of the organ of generation?

Rabbi Akiba responded to the Roman general by explaining that God left the creation incomplete, telling men to finish the work, so that we could become partners in His creation of the world.[11]

We are incomplete. Imperfect. And guilty. To become more complete and to be more perfect is precisely our role. To be goaded by our guilt to aspire and to achieve, that is man's opportunity in the world, an unending opportunity as long as we are alive.

Ontological imperfection must lead to psychological guilt. Psychological guilt presents problems, often soluble ones, that can improve our lives.

But that is not the only possibility. To our detriment, we may assume that, *were we worthy*, we would be perfect, as we should be. And because we are not perfect we may learn, again to our detriment, that we are bad. Constructed with consciences, we may live, therefore, with an unending sense of guilt, stymied and unable to crawl out of the deep holes we will have created for ourselves.

Were we to live with ontological guilt, then, the guilt itself would be the biggest stumbling block. Guilt would convince us that we are bad, flawed, and unable to change. Guilt would tempt us to radical actions that would require serious self-injury or the destruction of others. This is the great temptation which guilt presents, and to which it is all too likely we will succumb.

OPPOSING ONTOLOGICAL GUILT

The human psyche has a limited number of ways to respond to the psychological predisposition that creates feelings of guilt and a guilty conscience. Throughout the long span of human history, the weakness of human culture is precisely this: that guilt becomes the heavy weight that few can bear. Guilt becomes the interpretive tool that convinces man of his unworthiness. Guilt undermines hope, and guilt is a one-way ticket to despair.

But this is only one kind of guilt. Guilt also is the tool for self-correction. One of the central tasks on the agenda of Biblical religion, then, is to remind us that we human beings may go in two opposite directions as a result of the capacities we have to feel guilty. One direction digs down and undermines the spiritual structure of a human being. The other direction lifts up and raises a human being to his loftiest heights.

Work every day to remember what the Bible says in the first chapter of Genesis: that God looks and sees the world created with man and says, "It is very good."

You have to be reminded that you are essentially *very good* because it certainly does not always appear that way. Every morning I wake up and recite the ancient prayers that praise God for creating light and darkness. Praising God for the creation is something we do morning and evening because if you only take the evidence of what happens during the hours in between, you may become convinced that you should be depressed by the depravity that intrudes on every single day, by the imperfections and the evils that are so much a part of human life. You might come to feel that basically creation is flawed with evil and that it is impossible to believe in good.

That possibility must be constantly fought. On the festival of Rosh Hashanah, for example, a portion is read from Scripture which describes the binding of Isaac. Abraham, you remember, is told by God to take his son, his only son, Isaac, and to sacrifice him as an offering upon one of the mountains. Abraham, God's true servant, dutifully does as he is commanded. And innocent Isaac dutifully follows his father's wishes and is bound upon the altar, ready to be sacrificed to God.

Many explanations have been given for the inclusion of this passage in the High Holy Day liturgy. I would like to suggest that it reacts to a pattern well known in the ancient world. Human sacrifice was often performed to atone for man's sins. The profound sense of evil and its primordial devastating power required such large gestures in response.

But the Biblical story of Isaac's binding concludes by rejecting this option. God does not want human sacrifices. The Bible has a completely different sense of man's confrontation with evil. It rejects ontological evil and it substitutes a series of challenges and goads to encourage man to better his ways.

The inclusion of such a Scriptural passage in the liturgy is a way of saying: "Beware. You may be tempted to read your guilt feelings in the wrong way. You may be tempted to dwell on your evil creation and you may be tempted, therefore, into a line of reasoning and a religious response to the reality of guilt which you should reject."

God does not want an extraordinary sacrifice of a child. God wants us to change our ways.

And come the Day of Atonement, Yom Kippur, the theme returns once again. For in the Scriptural reading for this day we learn of the ancient Jewish practice of sending out a scapegoat that bears upon its head the sins of the people of Israel. Look what has happened to the extraordinary pagan practice. A person is not sent out. Not even an eye is plucked out. In line with the Biblical conceptions of sacrifice, a goat is sent away.

How tame in comparison. How relatively small a sacrifice.

It is in line with a wholly different conception of guilt and of evil. The emphasis is clear: Change your ways. Become better people. Consider the emotional motivations for your deeds and consider the rational need to control your actions. That is what God wants from man.

For there is a purpose to this gnawing, existential feeling of inadequacy that guilt causes. Its purpose is to cause each human being to change. To be better. To repent.

CHAPTER 13

Repent Before It Is Too Late

Great is repentance, for it brings men near to the Divine Presence. . . . But yesterday this person was odious before God, abhorred, estranged, an abomination. Today he is beloved, desirable, near, a friend.
—**Maimonides,** *Mishneh Torah, Laws of Repentance, 7:6*

I would far rather feel contrition than be able to define it.
—**Thomas à Kempis,** *The Imitation of Christ*

The desire to change and to chart a new path is a desire that most of us have. It may be in the form of a diet, or a switch from gin and tonic to chardonnay. It may be a search to rediscover the enchantment and the attachment you once had toward your wife. Or it may be an effort to fix up your relations with your father, your boss, or even the IRS. But sooner or later the bug that tempts you to make your life better will surely bite.

And you will look for the resources that make it possible for you to change.

Not very long ago that route was well marked and well known. It was called *repentance,* and people had access to their own inner resources through the spiritual traditions of their own religious faiths, so that they could repent and change. In this era, though, when religion no longer dominates, repentance—like guilt—exists for many in a realm somewhere between the quaint and the crazy. The cry, "Repent before it is too late," is the cry of an idiot, a sign displayed by a scruffy long-haired man in many a downtown that makes you want to cross the street.

Think, for example, how our terminology has changed. It wasn't so long ago that criminals served their time in a "penitentiary." (That is what we used to call a jail.) The word comes from the Latin root *penitentiarius,* a place to do penance. Maybe that fit the bill years ago, but today we are more matter-of-fact. We have "correctional institutions." No penitence, please, just correction—as if it were so easy to be correct, like adjusting the focus on a movie projector, and as if repentance, good old-fashioned repentance, did not have to play a crucial part.

But, even though the word has lost its luster, repentance—again, like guilt—is still around. This old-fashioned term deserves to be polished up. Even if not in so many words, people can—and do—repent. And, I hope you will agree, much can be learned by bringing this old classic back, unretouched, and not even colorized.

WHAT IS REPENTANCE?

How can we define repentance? The Hebrew term for it is *teshuvah,* which means "turning back" and carries with it the sense of returning to the point of departure after completing a full cycle. In the Bible, for example, you read of *teshuvat hashanah,* meaning the completion of the annual cycle of seasons.[1] Or, in another context, Scripture speaks of Samuel returning to his home in Ramah following a full round of visits to various towns in Israel.[2] Again, the same word, *teshuvah.* By extension, then, the Hebrew root is used to refer to a *return to God*.[3] The resonance, then, that is heard with the word is one of movement back. It implies, of course, that there is some place to go back to—that there is a point of reference and an anchorage which can resist the winds and shoals of many great storms.

Such a return takes place on two levels, and the act of repentance often connects these two levels in human life. They are external and internal. A penitent sinner is one who examines his ways, finds them wanting, and *changes his deeds*. As the prophet Isaiah was careful to ask:

> Is such the fast that I have chosen?
> The day for a man to afflict his soul?
> Is it to bow down his head as a bulrush,
> And to spread sackcloth and ashes under him?
> Wilt thou call this a fast,
> And an acceptable day to the Lord?
> Is not this the fast that I have chosen?
> To loose the fetters of wickedness,
> To undo the bands of the yoke,
> And to let the oppressed go free,
> And that ye break every yoke?
> Is it not to deal thy bread to the hungry,
> And that thou bring the poor that are cast out to thy house?
> When thou seest the naked, that thou cover him. . . .
> —Isaiah 58:5–7

Repentance is a turn in direction that leads to *doing better*.

But repentance is also a form of inner healing. It is a consequence of feeling debased and unworthy, of being less than a human being should be. It is a product of feeling self-contempt because of the state of one's life, a product of feeling polluted and impure. Repentance purifies and reroots a soul. Repentance reestablishes an inner harmony, a center of gravity, and a balance around which a human being can then freely move. Moreover, this inner experience is one that affirms the meaning of an individual's life and deeds. It is both a statement made and a commitment given to a cause, to a world of value which stands above every human being.

Repentance is an act, is *the* act of human freedom. It is the act that says "no" to the long chain of cause and effect that is behind each human act and that describes every person's past, and says: I am more than the sum of my past accomplishments. I am more than a total and complex picture of many stimuli and the history of responses to them. I am a unique human being and I assert my existence and its value by an act which is a free act, and one which, because it is so free, describes, more than any other description, just who I am.[4]

As Rabbi Adin Steinsaltz has explained: "The recognition of the need to turn comes about in different ways. Sometimes one is overcome by a sense of sinfulness, of blemish, of defilement, which results in a powerful desire for escape and purification. But the desire to turn can also take more subtle forms, feelings of imperfection or unrealized potential, which spur a search for something better."[5]

As a quest for purity, repentance is an effort to use self-analysis in the service of self-perfection, to use serious reflection in the service of spiritual purification—all in order to do away with the metaphysical corruption of the divine image in man.

These two goals, to *do* better and to *be* better, lead to two related but different tasks: to *repair broken relations with others*, the others sometimes being other people, other things (like nature, from the animals to the ozone, or, most importantly, God), and to *purify one's self*.[6] The guideposts that are part of this turning offer directions to make the act of repentance possible and effective. And it is the process of repentance, its several different steps and their impact on each individual, that provides the road map necessary for this turning to take place.

PRESIDENTIAL PENITENCE

The former president of South Korea has already pointed the way to resurrecting repentance. In a nationally televised speech in November 1988, former President Chun Doo-hwan of South Korea apologized to his nation for the corruption that marked his regime and asked forgiveness for the wrongs he committed against his people. Taking responsibility for the brutal government suppression of a 1980 revolt in which hundreds of civilians were killed, he surrendered $24 million worth of property as a gesture of his "atonement."

"It is more than unbearable for me to face you and make this confession of my shameful deeds, and I deeply apologize," Mr. Chun said. "The scar will be forever with me in my heart for the people who have suffered, and for this I feel more regret than I can express." He ended his half-hour address with a bow to his countrymen.

What an extraordinary scene! And a helpful one, too. For it had all the elements of repentance, and it carried with it all the doubts, as well. The elements we shall see shortly. But the doubts are important to note. Think: Will the people of South Korea forgive Mr. Chun for the excesses and corruption of his strongman rule because he has apologized? How would you react to a leader who had abused his power and publicly apologized? Would you be seeking more than mere words, even more than giving back some money? It makes you wonder who his PR man is and how much money he still has stashed away in some Swiss bank, doesn't it? On the other hand, the apparent humiliation of a public apology seems like welcome punishment for such awful crimes. But is it enough? Should there be some public punishment administered by those who had been wronged? Exile?

These are the kinds of questions that an act of repentance begins to raise in a person's mind. Even as the act seems profound and virtuous, you wonder whether it is at the same time corrupt. Or, as Friedrich Nietzsche claimed, you may wonder whether it is a form of inner deception.[7]

Do words really possess the power to change reality? Can they truly atone for wrongs that have so profoundly affected many people? The act of repentance, while seemingly humble, could possibly trivialize the very wrongs for which the wicked person has decided to atone—as if a few words could make up for all the suffering inflicted upon innocent people. Or is such an act, if freely given and truly meant, an act of contrition that is to be respected and an act of healing that can, in fact, help to heal past wounds?

Repentance is so extraordinary an act partly because it raises so many good questions. It seems to bear within itself such extraordinary possibilities: to change a person's sense of self. To clear an individual in others' eyes. To reestablish a harmonious relationship which had been destroyed because of someone's deeds. And yet, in the search for a morally appropriate response to wrongdoing, it is also true that repentance runs the danger of seeming puny—a lot of noise that really signifies nothing.

ALTERNATIVES TO REPENTANCE

Repentance, with its promise and its problems, has long been a challenge to religious life. The Talmud, for example, sees repentance as just one of the possible means for responding to evil deeds—a means that happens to be favored by God (and which therefore could not be more highly recommended), but a means that is not at all easy to accept.

How is the sinner punished? the Talmud asks. When the Books of Wisdom were asked this question, they replied: "Evil pursueth sinners" (Proverbs 13:21). You know that answer. Evil eventually will bring its own sorry reward to those who are forever locked in its clutches. Crime doesn't pay. An answer that is sometimes true—but how many evil people do you know who are paying? And paying the appropriate price?

When the Books of Prophecy were asked the same question, Prophecy replied: "The soul that sinneth, it shall die" (Ezekiel 18:4). Now that one is easier to like. It appeals to my blood-and-thunder moralistic sense. But it is a little extreme, is it not?

When the Torah was asked how the sinner is punished, the Torah replied: Let him bring an offering and he shall gain atonement, for it is written that "it shall be accepted for him to make atonement for him" (Leviticus 1:4). That is the answer of the religious throughout the generations—that the rituals of religion offer each person the symbolic means to satisfy his or her moral problems. If you pray hard enough, if you give enough charity, if you "bring your sacrifices," then your deeds will be forgiven. But what, I ask myself, of all the South Koreans whose lives have been ruined in the meantime? Will a little old-fashioned religion do the trick?

The Holy One was asked: How is the sinner punished? The

Holy One replied: Let him turn in repentance and he shall gain atonement, as it is written, "Good and upright is the Lord; therefore doth He instruct sinners in the way" (Psalms 25:8).[8]

What is the preferred method, God's method—forgetting the predilections of the Books of Wisdom, the prophets, and even the religious? Repentance. What, then, is the message that begs to be repeated? Simply, repent before it is too late!

Repentance is, from God's point of view, the peak human experience. "So great is repentance that it reaches the throne of glory."[9] It was created prior to the universe, according to the rabbis, [10] meaning that its preexistence made the world possible. You can see that we were not meant to come into this world as perfect creatures, not even as mindless creatures who would be forever without choice in determining their lives, but rather as human beings able, and even expected, to err. But erring is not final. Wrongdoing is not the last word about our lives. The last word is: repent. We can start over again, renewed, if we repent.

THE WAY TO REPENT

While there are many descriptions of the process of repentance, and many mixed brews that are said to work, they can all be distilled into five potent substrates that successfully bring about change, the five "R's" of repentance which make up five "Thou shalts." [11]

1. *Remorse*. Thou shalt . . . feel bad and be remorseful about what you have done.

2. *Recantation*. Thou shalt . . . turn feelings into words and confess your sins.

3. *Renunciation*. Thou shalt . . . willfully renounce your wrongdoings, removing them from your feelings and thoughts and deciding not to commit them again.

4. *Resolution*. Thou shalt . . . resolve to follow a better path in the future, to lift yourself up to where you want to be.

5. *Reconciliation*. Thou shalt . . . ask for forgiveness.

Let us see how these five "R's" work.

CHAPTER 14
The Way of Return

Guilt, we saw earlier on, has a dimension that is rooted in the emotions and a dimension that is rooted in the intellect. Guilt is a pain in the gut and a pain in the mind. The visceral pain of guilt finds its creative outlet in the catalytic feeling of remorse, a deeply emotional experience that induces profound change.

REMORSE

Remorse is an awful feeling inside that is connected to guilt. It indicates that you have not only told yourself that you have

141

done wrong but that the message is delivered especially viscerally: you feel a sense of revulsion toward yourself.

If a man hits his wife, he will, one hopes, feel remorse. If he has cheated on her, he will, one hopes, feel remorse. When a woman has beaten her child she will, one hopes, feel remorse. When a person has embezzled money, one hopes he will feel remorse.

In all of these cases, a sick feeling is an appropriate feeling to have. For in all of these cases, we find ourselves being carried away with the emotions of the moment and then committing acts which are deeply embarrassing to us.

People sometimes feel so guilty at these times that they take out their guilt by persecuting the members of their families. Because a man feels guilty about what he has done to his wife he will blame her for every possible sin under the sun. It appears as if he is trying to justify his wrong by making it seem as if she deserved what she got. What he is really doing is squirming with his guilt, unable to let down his guard long enough to take the blow of remorse to his body.

Strangely enough, though, it is only when that point comes, and when he feels cheapened, low, and horrible, that then, and only then, will he be able to transform the feelings that he has inside. Strangely enough, it is only when he has suffered sufficiently that he will be able to feel good once again. That good feeling may allow him to reestablish his relationship with his wife and to reestablish his self-respect. But until he arrives there, he will have a very difficult time.

Describing what is undoubtedly an extreme case, the Bible tells the story of Amnon's rape of Tamar (2 Samuel 13).[1] Amnon was King David's son, Tamar one of David's daughters, though each had a different mother. The Bible describes Amnon's infatuation with Tamar, a lust so great that it made him sick. He creates a ruse to be alone with Tamar. He overpowers her "and lay with her by force."

When the deed is done, however, Amnon "hated her with exceeding great hatred; for the hatred wherewith he hated her was greater than the love wherewith he had loved her." He is filled with disgust and the reader wonders: How can that be? Can passionate love turn so quickly into passionate hate?

The truth is that Amnon hates himself, not Tamar. He projects that hatred onto the victim of his lust. The object of his sinning now becomes the butt of his scorn.

Why? There is an instinctive feeling that operates within us that causes us to feel remorse. It is essentially an anti-esthetic experience, a feeling of disgust. Disgust at ourselves. Disgust at our deeds, disgust at our lives. Not a nice feeling, nothing lofty. Simply disgust. Yet the amazing reality is that such feelings can serve to transform the way a person is.

Amnon loses his lust. A husband loses his desire for a woman other than his wife. A mother suddenly finds it possible to transform her relations to her child, somehow turning her anger into tenderness, a tenderness which she is sure was always there but which never could adequately express itself. From remorse, a person can lose the motivation to sin. Through feelings—feelings of guilt that lead to remorse—a person can be renewed.

No doubt, too much remorse can be devastating. And the "therapeutic" benefit of remorse has its limits, of course. In the psychopathic personality, for example, remorse may be a passing phase of response to a terrible deed.

Hours before serial killer Ted Bundy was executed in January 1989, he was interviewed by James Dobson, a religious broadcaster and psychologist. Bundy was a forty-two-year-old law school dropout who was a bizarre mix of intelligence, charm, and sick, homicidal drives. Prodded by the interviewer to explore the sources of his violence, Bundy said that during his murder rampages he still felt, in his otherwise regular daily life, "the full range of guilt and remorse" about other things. "Each time I'd harm someone, each time I would kill someone, there would be an enormous amount, especially at first, an enormous amount of horror, guilt, remorse afterward, but then the impulse to do it again would come back. . . ."[2]

The exception does not, of course, mitigate the true power of remorse, but, like many an exception, it confirms the rule. Set against such a bizarre and sickly form of guilt, *normal* guilt, and the remorse which is associated with it, stands out in all its power and with all of its useful features.

The distance between remorse and depression may not be

great. But it is so important to ask: "Why do I feel so terrible? Is it some unexplainable psychological depression? Or, possibly, do I feel remorse for what I have done?"

If it is remorse, then we know that remorse can be itself a purgative feeling. Remorse is so powerful that it can utterly transform one's inner feelings. And what we simply must do is recognize what is going on in us. If we can be transformed, if we are on the brink of change, then let us not give in to either the temptation to be overly remorseful or to the temptation to reject the entire experience in our belief that guilt is bad for us.

Feeling remorseful is, therefore, step one.

RECANTATION

Remember, guilt is more than a feeling. It is a feeling that invades the realm of consciousness. That is why we begin with remorse. But the remorse has to lead to a careful, objective reflection upon what has happened to our lives. The second step, then, is recantation, which requires a verbal confession. The psalmist pictures this so perfectly:

> When I kept silence, my bones wore away
> Through my groaning all the day long.
> For day and night Thy hand was heavy upon me;
> My sap was turned as in the droughts of summer.
> I acknowledged my sin unto Thee, and mine iniquity have
> I not hid;
> I said: "I will make confession concerning my transgres-
> sions unto the Lord"—
> And Thou, Thou forgavest the iniquity of my sin.
> —Psalms 32:3–5

Silence was so painful. Even if a person roars all day long, in business or at home, keeping a perpetual curtain of silence drawn in front of the conscience that is heavy with guilt leads that person into feeling as if he is in the midst of a terrible drought, so thirsty is he for relief. What is the way out? Acknowledging sin and confessing transgressions.

"Whenever a man or woman commits any wrong toward a fellow man," says the Bible in the Book of Numbers (5:6–7), "thus breaking faith with the Lord, and that person realizes his guilt, he shall confess the wrong that he has done." Thus confession involves a level of self-contemplation in which feelings are verbalized.

At the same time, however, it is equally possible that we may sometimes repent by beginning with thoughts, by raising ideas in our own minds such as reciting a printed confessional: "Forgive us, our Father, for we have sinned. For the sin which we have committed by . . ." Fill in the blanks, recite the sins, and begin the thought process that may lead to confession.

Confession gets the feeling out, lessening the burden and putting it in a place where it can be more easily examined. It is both catharsis and the beginning of an intellectual process that renders the feelings that are deep inside us accessible, accessible to the powerful control of our wills in the next two steps of repentance: "renunciation" and "resolution." Before the will can touch them, though, the feelings need to be transformed into words.

The process of verbalizing guilt is a crucial process. It operates in sublime private moments of religious ecstasy but it can—and sometimes should—operate in public. Dennis Erickson, who is currently coach of the Washington State football team, has lamented over the way he left his former team, the Wyoming Cowboys. He got a fine offer for the job for which he had waited for a lifetime, and suddenly bolted. He had assured his team that he was staying with them, and then, without saying a word of goodbye, he was gone. "I still wake up at night in a cold sweat thinking about what I did," said Erickson. "I didn't leave the right way. If I had it to do over again, I would have returned to Laramie and told my players and the people what was going on. I was a young idiot. I didn't do it right."[3]

What didn't he do? Verbalize his guilt in the presence of those whom he felt that he had wronged.

People are often led, especially in extreme circumstances, to confess as a result of the remorse they feel. It is the only way to unburden the weight. Eighteen years after he killed twenty-one-year-old Lenore Mussenden, a college student, her killer confessed to the murder. He had been picked up on a shoplifting charge, and confessed to the officer who arrested him. Something had been "burdening" him, he told the officer, and he confessed to the killing. Said the Staten Island District Attorney, William L. Murphy, "I've heard about cases like this, but I've never had one. The chance something like this could happen is one reason murder is not bounded by the statute of limitations."[4]

You have to talk about your guilt. And the more complex the guilt is, the more necessary it is to find a workable context in which that guilt can, in fact, be revealed. That is why it is so helpful, in most religions, to unburden the soul by revealing hidden guilts to God. Psychotherapy and group therapeutic experiences can also serve this purpose, in some degree accounting for their popularity.

RENUNCIATION

Third comes renunciation. Repentance is, after all, an act of the will. Willpower is man's great gift. It is, at the same time, one of his weakest links with his higher self. As Rabbi Simhah of Przysucha (Poland, 1765–1827) put it: "Man's great guilt lies in the fact that he can turn away from evil at any moment, and yet he does not." Ergo, he lacks the will.

And what does guilt afford us more than the reminder that acts of will are possible? Ranging from the elemental willpower that fights against eating a piece of cake that may threaten an already endangered figure to the willpower necessary to fight the temptation of lust, from the will necessary to battle against the desire to accumulate material possessions regardless of whether they are ethically accumulated or not to the willpower that fights the temptation to procrastinate, all these are battles daily fought.

Renunciation involves using our will to abandon our sins. It is like a very sharp knife that cuts a rope that ties us down. All the desire in the world to change won't make any difference at all if the ropes of the past are not first cut.

Behind the entire period of penitence in the Jewish calendar beginning before the New Year and continuing through the Day of Atonement, there is a beautiful idea.

> Rabbi Kruspedai said in the name of Rabbi Yohanan: Three books are opened on Rosh Hashanah, one for the thoroughly wicked, one for the thoroughly righteous and one for the intermediate. The thoroughly righteous are forthwith inscribed definitively in the book of life; the thoroughly wicked are forthwith inscribed definitively in the book of death; the doom of the intermediate is suspended from Rosh Hashanah till Yom Kippur: if they deserve well, they are inscribed in the Book of Life; if they do not deserve well, they are inscribed in the Book of Death.[5]

That is to say, then, that acts of will are called for, with appropriate deadlines. And we assume that we all fall into the category of those who are "intermediate." And the "intermediates" are assigned to first cut the ropes.

Writing in the *New York Post*, Norman Podhoretz advises the new "drug czar," William J. Bennett, to learn from the difficult experience he is likely to face in breaking a smoking habit.[6] The very dependence that Mr. Bennett has for nicotine and the willpower that he will have to muster in order to overcome that dependence will teach him a great deal about what addicts are like. "And so in the end," says Podhoretz, "I come out with a strong endorsement of the much-ridiculed slogan of Nancy Reagan's campaign against drugs: 'Just say no.' "

Mr. Bennett may feel guilty about smoking. Addicts may feel guilty about taking drugs. But without willpower, there is little possibility for change.

RESOLUTION

Remorse over past actions, confessions, and a renunciation of past deeds is a prelude to another willful act, a resolution and commitment regarding the future. Maimonides puts it this way:

"What is repentance? That a sinner abandon his sin, remove it from his mind, and commit himself to not do it again." [7]

It is the commitment toward the future that marks this level of repentance. For there are two time frames in which the will can work. It can make decisions about the past. It can make judgments regarding what has been done. But the will works most potently when it makes a commitment for the time that is to come. It is this resolution that characterizes most people's sense of what repentance is all about. It is the New Year's resolution. The birthday resolution. The diet resolution. The family resolution. Now I will be the kind of person I have not been able to be until this point. But now, it will work!

Repentance must reach this stage. "To feel discomfort and explain it away with a shrug, or any number of verbal equivalents, may not lead to even the decision to change, let alone change itself. On the other hand, genuine regret for one's misdeeds and recognition of one's failings do not necessarily lead to the desired outcome either; instead, they can cause a deepening sense of despair and a fatalistic resignation. . . . Thus remorse alone, however decisive it may be initially, must be accompanied by something else: belief in the possibility of change. In this sense, the principle of *teshuvah*—that no matter what the starting point, no matter how far gone the sinner, penitence is possible—is itself an important source of reawakening and hope." [8]

This is, frankly, the most difficult aspect of repentance, the place where most people fail. According to a recent study, "nearly half of more than 200 people studied failed to keep their New Year's resolutions for a month, and less than one in five followed their pledges for two years." [9] These "failures" are not alone. Every one of us could surely join their ranks.

It is the test of our true intentions—and don't we know that it is a test that is hard to pass! Habit, which may have caused the problem in the first place, is very difficult to change.

RECONCILIATION

The fifth step toward repentance is reconciliation. Reconciliation with others is attained through seeking their forgiveness, and he who is forgiven is a happy person. As the Psalmist says, "Blessed is he whose transgression is forgiven, whose sin is covered." [10]

We need to be forgiven by someone outside ourselves because the transgressions we commit, the wrongdoings that lead to our guilty feelings, are to a great extent committed upon others. Others are injured by us. The harmonious relationships that *should* exist between a man and his wife, between children and their parents, between friends and co-workers, between leaders and the citizens who are their followers—all of these relationships are hurt, sometimes even destroyed, by virtue of the injuries we inflict upon others. And, it goes without saying that most of our discussion about guilt is precisely about the guilty feelings and the guilty conscience that result from hurting others.

This is true, as we shall see, in several different relationships —most importantly in our relations with other people, and, not incidentally, in our relationship with God. In both cases, sin leads to unpleasant consequences, and, therefore, part of the process of repentance involves the reestablishment of love between the offended parties. It involves, it demands an effort to reach out to another, to a friend, to a loved one, to God, and to say, I am sorry. Please forgive me for what I have done.

The act of asking forgiveness is a statement that one is willing to cast aside one's arrogance, to debase one's self enough so that you *come crawling* if necessary. It is an experience that, in its extreme and unpleasant form, can be an experience of humiliation. From this standpoint, an apology derives its importance from the pain it produces.

An apology is public. As long as you are apologizing to someone else, you can't do it all by yourself. It is a humbling experience and there is a level of embarrassment that can smart. In fact, it is these characteristics that have led some to suggest that an apology is an effective way of punishing a crime and even of deterring future wrongdoing.

In Tampa, Florida, for example, a prosecutor has criminals apologize for their crimes in newspaper advertisements as punishment, in return for probation and dropping of some minor charges. "I've admitted my guilt . . . I've been punished. It wasn't worth it. I'm sorry," said an ad purchased by one man. He was given a public apology option, and he bought small advertisements in the local newspaper.

John Skye, chief of the felony division in the state attorney's office, believes the embarrassment of a public apology can be an effective tool. "It's a public act of contrition that is unpleasant to do and thus can act as a deterrent, similar to going to jail," he said.

The sociologist Dr. Amitai Etzioni has gone so far as to suggest that "Public humiliation is a surprisingly effective and low-cost way of deterring criminals and expressing the moral order of a community. It is used by a few judges, but much too sparingly."

Etzioni's social science colleagues react to such public humiliations with horror, feeling them to be dehumanizing and a violation of people's basic rights. But, he responds, what are the alternatives? Jailing is bad, especially for first-time offenders. In addition to being expensive, it brings criminals into contact with the worst possible elements for their own good. Public humiliation involves no socializing with other criminals, is swift and low cost.

AN APOLOGY ASKS FOR LOVE

But what is the real purpose of an apology? To limit its use to its humbling deterrent value is to miss the true emotion that it is designed to elicit. It is principally a way of asking for love, and, by doing so from a position of weakness, it is precisely the kind of request that is most likely to elicit from someone else a powerful, loving response in return.

Reconciliation is a necessary part of the process of repentance. I suspect that even if one did not bring God or another person into the picture, it could be argued that reconciliation would still be necessary for a person to come to live with himself. But especially because of the fact that someone else is implicated, it would be insufficient to simply *regret* the wrongful action. It would be insufficient even to be remorseful because of what one has done. A confession of wrongdoing would be interesting, but even this would not be enough.

After all, of what significance would such self-centered analysis be? Someone else has been hurt, and therefore someone else deserves to be approached.

Therefore the great penitential days of the Jewish year, Rosh Hashanah, the New Year, and Yom Kippur, the Day of Atonement, both concentrate on the need to achieve forgiveness, forgiveness from God for the transgressions of the year past, and forgiveness from fellow human beings.

Furthermore, reconciliation requires that atonement take into account the appropriate restitution that is due in a particular case. Where monetary fraud is involved, for example, remorse will not bring atonement until the embezzled money is restored to its lawful owner.[11] One cannot clear his religious conscience while "civil" or monetary claims are still pending.

GUILT AND CHANGE

These five "R's" of repentance constitute a psychology of change. And they bring into focus the way that guilt can induce such change.

Rabbi Israel Salanter, one of the great rabbis of the nineteenth century, preceded Sigmund Freud when he wrote of two sources responsible for each person's behavior. One is conscious and operates through the medium of the intellect. The other is unconscious and operates through the inner world of the emotions. They are both important, though not to the same degree, for behavior has its deepest roots, he felt, in the unconscious emotional side of life.

According to Rabbi Salanter, various means exist to control behavior, each of which is a response to this two-sided understanding of human psychology. It is possible, he felt, to *subdue* one's evil tendencies. That is the task of the intellect: to reach certain conclusions about what correct behavior is and to use the power of the intellect to effectuate change. This is much like Plato's picture, where the mind acts as a control; it holds the reins and makes sure the horses of passion do not go astray.

But, Rabbi Salanter goes on, there is a higher level of transformation that should be the true goal of a sensitive human being. *Tikun hamidot, perfecting,* and not just controlling, behav-

ior, is that higher goal. This perfection results from going beyond an external control of passions. It transforms the passions
themselves. It *transmutes* the motivation to sin and thereby truly
succeeds in transforming a human being.[12] But such transformation is possible only when the unconscious sources of behavior are attacked. Only through the emotions can evil be
abolished rather than merely held back.

On both these levels, guilt operates at the cutting edge. The
conscious level of affecting behavior is what we call conscience.
The unconscious and emotional level that affects behavior is
easily understood by *feeling* guilty.

What reaches the control centers of behavior with great
power? What is found at the meeting place between the moral
imagination and the emotional unconscious? Guilt.

It is guilt that is the door to many of these conscious and
emotional centers of behavior. It is, in fact, guilt that is the
experiential locus of the moral and potentially transmutable
human being. It is guilt, therefore, that can act as a catalyst, as
a *good* catalyst, to induce positive behavioral change.

DOES REPENTANCE WORK?

But does it all work? Of course it does, even though successful change is hard to achieve. Let the repentant speak:

Reverend Jeb Magruder, the convicted Watergate conspirator
turned Presbyterian minister, says that his past was the perfect
preparation for his new post as head of Columbus, Ohio's,
Commission on Values and Ethics.[13] At first this seems like
inviting the fox into the henhouse to take his turn at being
guard. Not so, says Magruder, who argues that studying ethics
from a theological perspective has affected his personal ethics.
"If they haven't changed, then it has been a real waste of time,
hasn't it?"

Exhibit number two: a Boston-based foundation called the
Haymarket People's Fund. Founded in 1974 by George Pills-
bury, an heir to the baking fortune, its purpose is, on the surface, to bankroll social change. At the same time, however, the
contributors to the fund are rich young people struggling with

the guilt of having large inheritances. Charles Schock, one of the board members of a similar San Francisco fund, the Threshold Foundation, describes a "rap session on money" during which one young inheritor stood up crying and said he felt as if he had "survivor's guilt." These people feel guilty for being rich and they try to assuage this guilt and consequently make themselves feel better about themselves by acting on their guilt and giving money away. Again, guilt leads to positive change.

BACK TO KOREA

And what, then, about former President Chun Doo-hwan of South Korea, who went to his countrymen via television and apologized for his corrupt regime? Will his repentance work? Far be it from me to prognosticate about that. But I can tell you that on the surface he made a decent try. He claims remorse, though, from what I have read, I would not want to weigh how much he felt. He confessed, and I do hope that the act of confession made him realize that he had done many wrong things. And, yes, he did apologize.

But the bottom line is: Did he really mean it? You cannot repent, after all, with half a heart. And you have to be able to communicate to the one you have wronged and be convincing at that. Whether the former president of Korea was successful on that score, I suppose that we will only know with time.

But he didn't do it a day too soon. Rabbi Eliezer said in the Talmud: " 'Repent one day before your death.' His disciples asked: 'But does man know the day of his death?' Rabbi Eliezer responded: 'This is exactly why he should repent today.' "[14]

CHAPTER 15

Loving Yourself Even Though You Are Less Than You Should Be

What other dungeon is so dark as one's own heart! What jailer so inexorable as one's self!
—**Nathaniel Hawthorne,**
The Blithedale Romance

Le moi est haissable. (The self is hateful.)
—**Blaise Pascal,** *Pensées*

I do plainly and ingenuously confess that I am guilty of corruption, and do renounce all defense. I beseech your Lordships to be merciful to a broken reed.
—**Francis Bacon,** *On being charged by Parliament with corruption in office*

One time, a month before the days of penitence that mark the New Year, Rabbi Levi Yitzhak of Berditchev (who died in 1810) stood looking out of his window. A cobbler passed by and asked him, "Have you nothing to mend?"

At once the rabbi sat himself down on the ground and, weeping bitterly cried, "Woe is me, and alas my soul, for the Day of Judgment is almost here, and I have still not mended myself." [1]

Self-mending is the first task of repentance. And unfortunately the cobbler can't do it for us. We have to examine our own lives and we ourselves also have to fix them up.

It is easier (or so it seems, at least) to figure out what is wrong with someone else. Pondering the imperfections of the neighbor next door or the colleague who works down the hall is a lot more appealing than thinking about our own. Pondering the imperfections of the mayor, the members of Congress, or the President is a delightful pastime, as well as the raw material that keeps editorialists busy. There is always a pair of shoes to mend—usually shoes that go on someone else's feet.

But, to echo Rabbi Levi Yitzhak, "Woe is me." How do we repair ourselves? This process of repentance begins with each person, wherever he is, wherever she is.

It is no easy task. First of all because the process of self-analysis is so disappointing. You get a good look, sometimes a surprising look, at how your soles are worn out. You remind yourself that you are imperfect, and that you often fail. And then, commonly, you say: How could I love that sorry specimen?—bringing to mind Groucho Marx's quip that he wouldn't want to join any club that would have him as a member!

How can you love yourself even though you are less than you should be?

And if that question weren't difficult enough, there is another that complicates the matter. Just who is this person I call "me"?

GETTING YOURSELF TOGETHER

Rabbi Hanokh, a Hasidic rabbi of the nineteenth century, put the difficulty this way:

"There once was a man who was very stupid. When he got

up in the morning it was so hard for him to find his clothes that at night he almost hesitated to go to bed, thinking of the trouble he would have on waking. One evening he finally made a great effort, took paper and pencil, and as he undressed, noted down exactly where he put everything he had on. The next morning, very well pleased with himself, he took the slip of paper in his hand and read: 'cap'—there it was, he set it on his head; 'pants' —there they lay, he got into them; and so it went until he was fully dressed.

" 'That's all very well, but now where am I myself?' he asked in great consternation. 'Where in the world am I?' He looked and looked, but it was a vain search; he could not find himself. 'And that is how it is with us,' said the rabbi.'' [2]

It is difficult to locate yourself. Even when you know where all the parts are, you still may not know where the self is that is really greater than the sum of its parts. There is an image that may or may not be you, and just how do you know?

Often, for example, a woman goes into a dress department to be outfitted for the new season, and she is greeted by the salesperson's deadpan assurance and confident proclamation: "That dress is *you*." How astonishing! the woman thinks. Was it me last year in miniskirts? Will it be me next year in tunics and pants? Would the real me please stand up?

Hardly anyone is immune to this dilemma, even the famous and the great. A man who purchased one of Pablo Picasso's paintings is said to have asked the master to vouch for the painting's authenticity. Picasso took one look and declared, "It is definitely a fake." The man was thunderstruck. He had paid a fortune for the painting and had been assured by all the critics that it was a true Picasso. "How," he said to the master, "can that be? I have a guarantee from the gallery that it was certainly painted by you." Picasso answered, "Well, I am sure that that is true. But all of my paintings are fakes."

The artist was well aware that there is a level of self-disclosure which is filled with self-delusion. And the search for the true self must therefore deal with the all too true anomaly that some of what we think expresses us best will turn out to be, upon analysis, only one of our paintings, and that one a "fake."

I hasten to add that not everyone will admit to the difficulty of knowing himself. Salvador Dali, Picasso's countryman, felt quite differently. Isabel Dufresne, who is writing a book about Dali, wrote immediately after his death of a dinner she had shared with the artist in a restaurant. "An obese lady, leaving the restaurant, stopped at our table. She said, 'Of course, I know who you are.' To which Dali replied: 'So do I.' " Alas, only the arrogant are granted such certainty!

Failure. Failure to be perfect. Failure even to locate all the clothes we need to put on to make an attempt at repentance work. But before we get carried away and are tempted to agree with Pascal and call the self hateful, remember:

You are imperfect. You must be imperfect. God created you imperfect. Get it through your head: there is no way to change this fact. You are an ontological misfit.

But you can still be better. You can change your ways.

And, as a matter of fact, the very disappointments you feel are the very best preparation for making these changes take place.

HE WHO WEEPS FINDS HIMSELF

Every imperfect person is created by God—no small matter, I must stress. Every imperfect person is very good—meaning that he has the innate capacity to make himself worthy of his creator's investment, even if he is not perfect. And not only that: every imperfect person has the task and the talent to minister to God as if he or she were a priest of old.

And do you know what were the high and unforgettable moments in the life of none other than the high priest?

The Talmud describes the procedures followed by the high priest on the night before the Day of Atonement. That was the night preceding the entry by the high priest into the holy of holies. There he would seek atonement for himself, for his family, and for the entire nation.

That night, the elders would come before him to review the procedures of the coming day. They would adjure him to heed their words, saying, "Alter nothing of what we have said to you." When the high priest heard their words, the Talmud says that he wept. And when the elders saw him weeping, they wept, too.[3]

The high priest wept? Wouldn't you think that he who wore so important a crown would be inured to his upcoming tasks? That he would have the bearing of his office and the importance of his ego to fortify him when he came before God?

Yet when he realized what he was going to do, his regal bearing collapsed. When he thought of his own sins, and the likelihood that he could not carry out his tasks as assigned, his demeanor was shattered and he cried.

You see, to go into the holy of holies, you first have to weep. You have to spend some time thinking about the fact that you feel like a failure when you begin to measure yourself against God's plan.

When a human being considers the responsibilities on his shoulders, the imperfections in his abilities, the stray places to which his heart runs, the failures that have marked him in the year past, it is time first to weep.

The late Professor Abraham Joshua Heschel once told a group of his students, "We are all failures. At least once a year," he went on, "we should all recognize it."

As every day passes, as days turn into weeks and weeks turn to months and years, we think that we could have done so much. But where are we now? Since a year ago, we have aged a year, and we now have less time, a year's worth of fewer options, to reach the goals we have in our lives.

Who is not aware of those he loves, of his family and friends, who are gone from this earth? Of the fact that he can no longer share their company, comfort their sorrows, encourage their strivings, and dance with them to celebrate their joys? And what a disappointment it is to think of what he might have done, what he might have said, had he realized the time was to be so short.

In any year, our children have grown older by what can only be called leaps and bounds. What a marvel it is to see how their bodies and their minds have matured. How extraordinary to think of the blessings we have shared with them. And yet, at the same time, every year has its disappointments that begin right at home. Disappointments that come from seeing that our children are not striving to realize our most important dreams. Disappointments that come from what they have done or not done. And disappointments, even worse, when we realize how we have failed them.

Laying on the guilt? Sure. What good parent doesn't feel guilty when it comes to a child? Oh, yes, you couldn't choose their jobs, you couldn't make them marry the person that was right for them. But when your children hurt, you hurt. Because they are still your babies, no matter what their age. Parents live with a magnifying lens that they place on the fabric of their children's lives; and, ultimately, what parent doesn't feel, when he looks at his child and sees what he doesn't like, that he has failed?

In any year, our mothers and fathers, if we are still blessed to have them, have aged. Some of them have become increasingly frail, and we have found ourselves filled with questions, frustrations, and disappointments about what our role should be as they grow older. How do we live with the decision we made to place Mother in a home, when there seemed to be no other decent way? How do we justify not having visited more often since we have been separated by so many miles? We love them and respect them, yet, here too, it is so hard to face so many difficult quandaries, that many of us feel we have failed.

We work years to build up not only our domestic lives, but our professional lives, trying to achieve success. Yet, inevitably, in every year there are dashed hopes there, too. Promotions that did not come, plans for expansion that evaporated into thin air. Opportunities that were lost. So many problems caused by economic conditions beyond our control, but which may make us feel that *we* have failed.

We live in a success-oriented country. Americans search always for success, and yet the lives of people are filled with many defeats. So much so that the Massachusetts Institute of Technology taught a course a few years ago on failure as "a dominating theme in society." But who needs to take the course? I am sure we could all stay home for the first few lectures. We know what failures are!

The rabbis point out that we are vessels of clay made by a

potter. Clay vessels, according to the Torah, can acquire ritual impurity, which makes them unfit to bring into holy places. How do you purify a clay vessel? By breaking it. Then it becomes pure.

So it is for human beings. Rarely does Judaism preach the *need* for suffering. But making a change in your life, deciding to enter the holy of holies, reaching up for a new level of purity, puts you face to face with your shortcomings.

If what you see in the mirror is a tarnished image, do as the high priest did. Open your heart and weep. Remember the words of the psalmist: "The sacrifices of God are a broken spirit: a broken and a contrite heart, O God, Thou wilt not despise" (Psalms 51:19).

Strangely enough, the steps that lead to loving yourself begin at the same place where all repentant acts begin: with remorse. A good cry is also a good start.

"I SHALL NOT DO THIS AGAIN"

In a sermon delivered on the Day of Atonement years ago, Rabbi Milton Steinberg asked the question: "What shall we do with our persistent and repeated failures?"[4] There are answers, he says, that people commonly give. The realist, for example, says that we regularly set our goals too high. Lower the goals, and we will not fail. But, says Rabbi Steinberg, with each failure and with each compromise of our ideals, there is less left for us to reach.

The cynic, on the other hand, counsels that ideals are delusions and, even worse, sources of discontent. Abandon them, and have peace at last. And that, of course, is peace achieved at the highest possible price.

Rabbi Steinberg finally concludes that the best response to failure is the view of Rabbi Levi Yitzhak of Berditchev, who was, you remember, so overcome when asked for shoes to mend. When Levi Yitzhak became old, he adopted the following practice. Each night, before he went to bed, he would review the events of the day that had passed. And he would say of whatever was evil in it, "I shall not do this again." Having looked at his deeds, and having said this, he would say to himself, "But so you promised last night and the night before." "Ah, yes," he would answer himself, "but tonight I am in earnest."

How could it be? Wasn't the rabbi just fooling himself? He was not.

He was committed to the path of repentance and took the only possible route. The first step he took was the step of *recantation*. He confessed his misdeeds. He kept a running tally and he looked at it every night. He put his moral life into perspective and he declared the legitimacy of giving it some thought.

That is the first and most important step that so many people never take. They know that it is hard to bring up children. They know that it is hard to be married to the same person for most of your life. They know that so many ethical decisions in business are gray rather than black and white. But, so often, recognizing the difficulties causes people to be instantly demoralized. They say simply: Because it is difficult to know what is right, it makes no difference at all. They abandon the ship the moment the water gets rough.

One of the most important reflective moments that each of us has is the moment when he says in all seriousness, "Hey, how am I doing?" It is a precious moment, one that should be multiplied every day of one's life. Keeping a daily log of your expenses is something that you may have learned to do in deference to the Internal Revenue Service. Why not keep a daily log of the obligations that you owe to a higher authority? Save part of your date book to keep this account—or find a place to enter it into your computer. And even if you fail day after day after day, your tally will remind you of what is important so that you will not fail even more than you do—and so that you will continue to steer by the right star.

When a new morality is declared by the media, you will have some reference to an old morality. You will be able to check the points of your compass so that you will be able to know just where you are and you will be able to accurately plot where you are to go. When a new chance to make money occurs to you, or to the financial wizards of the day, you will have some standards that will impel you, even unconsciously, to ask yourself, "Is this an ethical idea?" All that from a repeated recitation of your failures. Feeling guilty about them is good.

And you will come to realize—slowly but surely it will work —that you can indeed change. You will find the strength to *renounce* what you have done in the past. And you will find the resources to *resolve* to change. It is simply not true that we never change. Yes, we need to sharpen our wills, but that being done, a change can, and often does, take place.

Sometimes it is a breakthrough that we could hardly have expected. We have been stingy in our charity for years and years. And finally we see a person in need who helps us break through. A young woman sleeping on the streets who could be your daughter or mine. A man with AIDS who is the son of someone you know. A destitute family traveling to the other side of the world to seek freedom in a new land. Someone's heartbreak becomes ours. Our mercy is stirred. Someone's need becomes a chance to do what we have never done before. Breakthroughs occur.

How often do I come back from the cemetery with people who declare, "My life is different today." When they gaze at the cold ground that now envelops their dear ones they discover a newfound warmth. A newfound humanity. A newfound purpose. Yes, breakthroughs take place.

But they need to be nurtured every day. That is why Rabbi Levi Yitzhak was so right. Every night is not too often. And even if tonight is no different from last evening, then after tomorrow night, or three hundred or three thousand nights from now, a dawn will finally break.

I FORGIVE MYSELF

The last step is reconciliation. To love yourself, even though you are less than you should be, you must forgive yourself.

We usually think of forgiving someone else. But as hard as that is, it is easier than forgiving yourself. Who knows better than you do just how many faults you have and what they are?

Who knows what is hidden? Only you and God. And neither offers escape.

Paul Tillich, the great Protestant theologian, writes of the overwhelming existential loneliness that afflicts each of us, and how we are ultimately closed into a room with ourselves. "Who has not," he writes, "at some time, been lonely in the midst of a social event? The feeling of our separation from the rest of life is most acute when we are surrounded by it in noise and talk. We realize then much more than in moments of solitude how strange we are to each other, how estranged life is from life. Each one of us draws back into himself. We cannot penetrate the hidden centre of another individual: nor can that individual pass beyond the shroud that covers our own being. Even the greatest love cannot break through the walls of the self." [5]

We are therefore alone and lonely, and there are limits to what we can expect from others. All the more reason, then, to remember that every self is created by God. Each is in His image. And that does not mean that only the selves that are good are so created, that only the saints are accepted as human beings and as children of the Most High. Every self can become good. Never perfect, never at the end of the becoming. But every moving, surging spirit in every sinful human being is a spirit that reflects God's concern.

And if we are good enough for God to be concerned, then shouldn't we feel good enough to deserve self-respect?

Imperfection may be troubling, but for God's children it is insufficient reason for despair.

My friend Rabbi Pesach Krauss wrote a beautiful book that is a helpful resource for people who are trying to cope with grief and with terrible losses. [6] In it, Rabbi Krauss describes his own youth, a youth made difficult by the fact that he was run over by a streetcar when he was three years old and had to have his right leg amputated just below the knee.

Wearing a prosthesis, he became a fanatical athlete, playing sports with a vengeance and trying to prove his self-worth every day on the ball field. The problem was that, no matter how well he did, he couldn't be as good as the other kids. He had set an impossible goal for himself.

But he did achieve great success. He won extraordinary victories as a gymnast even though he had only one good leg. He eventually won an athletic scholarship to college. And Rabbi Krauss learned a lot about himself.

In his sophomore year in high school, he made the school gymnastics team. Proudly he walked down the hallway wearing the bulky red wool sweater that had on it his school's letter. He walked into his homeroom, bursting with pride. He writes:

> Inside the classroom, the other kids stopped their chatter and turned to stare at me. Krauss, the kid with the gimpy leg. . . . What was that he was wearing? A hush came over the room. And then an amazing thing happened.
>
> In unison, all my classmates rose. They began to clap their hands. Softly at first. Then louder. And they cheered.
>
> I'm not ashamed to tell you that on that day, standing there in front of my classmates, the tears I cried were the sweetest tears of all.
>
> For the first time I had a glimmer that I could be a whole person even if part of me is missing.[7]

Because he felt loved. Because he felt accepted. He felt as whole as anyone could be. *Even if he didn't have two of his own legs.*

This is the crucial test that we face in spiritual life, too. Here it begins by each of us becoming aware of how imperfect we are. That awareness helps us to break through the emotional barriers that keep us from changing ourselves. To do all that and not get so wrapped up in ourselves that we are convinced that we are the greatest. And to do all that and not be convinced that we are the lowliest worms upon the earth.

As we have seen, forgiveness implies a state of crawling. It is a humbling experience. Yet self-forgiveness brings out another dimension. That we will cheer for ourselves even in those moments when no one else is around to applaud. Self-forgiveness means that we are ultimately loved and accepted. That our lives are good and complete beyond our comprehension. And that they are grounded in an endless love.

"Simply accept the fact that you are accepted," Paul Tillich says. "In that moment, grace conquers sin, and reconciliation bridges the gulf of estrangement. And nothing is demanded . . . but acceptance," to accept oneself as accepted in spite of being unacceptable.[8]

COUNT YOUR BLESSINGS, TOO

Repentance requires a "pick-me-up." In his book *The Lights of Penitence*, Rabbi Abraham Isaac Hacohen Kook suggests that while penitence has eliminated a virus from a person's existence, it also will weaken his healthy vitality.[9] It is because of that, he notes, that the penitential season of the Jewish year is followed by the festival of Sukkot, days of holy joy and gladness that revivify the self.

Help yourself to feel good, and you will help yourself to repent. If you are feeling guilty, go out and do something nice for yourself. If you are depressed because of your moral state, don't leave it at that, but have your hair done, or buy yourself a new pair of shoes. A hard hand needs to be balanced by one that is soft. A slap hurts; it needs lots of self-love in return.

Don't expect too little of yourself. But don't expect too much, too soon, either. Be sensitive to your own proclivities and natural predispositions: Some people are endowed from birth with great spiritual energy, and they leap and change radically when they repent. Others rise through good deeds and study. They must progress slowly.[10]

That we are meant to be good is a fact that is a blessing. And until we count our blessings we may get hung up on the measure of our faults. Not so that we can say how glorious and good we are. Not so that we can inflate our egos so that we fly off like balloons. But just so that we maintain a sense of proportion. So that we remember that we are blessed in many ways. And so that we will be able to be grateful for our lives, and feel good rather than bad.

"Life is ever surprising," writes Jane Vonnegut Yarmolinsky. She had been living the life of a struggling writer's wife until a fateful day in 1958 when her brother-in-law was killed when a New Jersey commuter train went off a bridge. A day and a half later, this man's wife died of cancer, and Jane Vonnegut Yarmolinsky and her then husband decided to bring their four orphaned nephews into their home. She writes of the years of trial and triumph that then ensued.

And when she gets to the end of the book, she tells her readers that she, herself, has cancer. She concludes:

> So what is there to say when you know you don't have much time left? Or rather, what is most important to say, since you can't say it all? I wrote this partly to find out what I might have to say. And in the doing I have discovered how absolutely madly in love I am with life and with all the people I was given—yes, given—to love. I am grateful to have learned so much of life: of the steadiness of personalities, the constancy of love, the preciousness of the moment, the fragility of time, the power of the imagination, the strength of that vital life force that enables us to hold each other up when our wings get broken. And perhaps, above all, I've learned that pain and joy are inextricably mingled, and that out of suffering does come love. It is a great mystery to me why this should be so.
>
> But I know that there will be angels in the next underpass as well, and I am content.[11]

Jane Vonnegut Yarmolinsky died before her manuscript was published. But she drank deeply of life, deeply from a cup that was often filled with bitter brew. She learned to taste her blessings, and to be grateful for them. She was therefore able to finally find herself, to put all of the pieces together and to conclude that her life was good.

Is that not the goal of repentance? To recover purity, and to feel that you are worthy to enter the holy of holies when the time comes?

Every day is a blessing and a gift. Who has received this gift? You have. You must be pretty good to have received that! You will count your blessings and you will say: Things are not all bad nor am I. And you will give yourself the self-confidence that you need to be able to purify your spirit and to change your ways.

CHAPTER 16

Loving Another Person Even When That Person Is Never What He or She Should Be

Rabbi Hayyim of Zans had married his son to the daughter of Rabbi Eliezer. The day after the wedding he visited the father of the bride and said: "Now that we are related I feel close to you and can tell you what is eating at my heart. Look! My hair and beard have grown white, and I have not yet atoned!" "O my friend," replied Rabbi Eliezer, "you are thinking only of yourself. How about forgetting yourself and thinking of the world?"
—Martin Buber, "The Way of Man, According to the Teachings of Hasidism"

> *Mine is a most peaceable disposition.*
> *My wishes are: a humble cottage with a*
> *thatched roof, but a good bed, good food,*
> *the freshest milk and butter, flowers*
> *before my window, and a few fine trees*
> *before my door; and if God wants to*
> *make my happiness complete, he will*
> *grant me the joy of seeing some six or*
> *seven of my enemies hanging from those*
> *trees. Before their death I shall, moved in*
> *my heart, forgive them all the wrong*
> *they did me in their lifetime. One must,*
> *it is true, forgive one's enemies—but not*
> *before they have been hanged.*
> **—Heinrich Heine,**
> *Gedanken und Einfalle*

While it is true that each of us would feel guilty even were we to be alone in this world, other people create vast new frontiers for guilt. Compared to the bad feelings generated by not living up to our ideals—feelings which usually come and go—guilt produced from disappointing our children or our parents, our husbands, wives, and co-workers is guilt that is a growth business. It is recession-proof.

Other people save us from being alone. Other people also give us reason to be guilty. And other people, because they have wronged us, are the objects of our anger and precisely those who should be feeling guilty for what they have done.

Which leaves us, ultimately, having to live with relationships that are less than perfect at best, and that are ruinous at worst. We have already looked at part of the picture of imperfection, at our own part: living with ourselves when we are far from perfect. And we have already spoken about what to do when we are at fault, hurting others: to let guilt be our guide in choosing actions that will heal. But what does it take to live with and to love another person who hurts us, another person who is never, and never will be, all that he or she should be?

THE SEARCH FOR A PERFECT PERSON

First, Sherlock, put down the magnifying lens you are using to find that perfect number ten. No one is perfect, and only if you haven't been able to extrapolate that conclusion about other people from what you see when you look in the mirror, or from the ten thousand pain-in-the-neck disappointments that have been served up to you by your friends, let alone your enemies, is it worth picking up that lens once again. Mr. Wonderful and his female counterpart, whether as a potential spouse, friend, representative in the U.S. Congress, or candidate for Miss America, is not, never was, and never will be perfect. That perfect person exists just the way fairies and goblins exist.

In a short story entitled "The Birth-mark," Nathaniel Hawthorne describes a passionate scientist who falls in love with and then marries a very beautiful woman. She would have been perfect, had it not been for a birthmark on her cheek. "It was the fatal flaw of humanity," writes Hawthorne, "which Nature, in one shape or another, stamps ineffaceably on all her productions, either to imply that they are temporary and finite, or that their perfection must be wrought by toil and pain."

But the scientist could not live with the defect in his wife. He creates a potion with the unique properties necessary to remove the blemish and, after administering it to his wife, rejoices to find that her blemish disappears. The story then concludes:

"As the last crimson tint of the birth-mark—that sole token of human imperfection—faded from her cheek, the parting breath of the now perfect woman passed into the atmosphere, and her soul, lingering a moment near her husband, took its heavenward flight."

The beautiful woman dies, because no one can live and be perfect. Only God is perfect, and man cannot even see God and live—let alone be God and live.

Point number one is: Don't expect perfection of anyone. Not of your husband or your wife, not of your children, not of your parents, not of your president, not of anyone.

ROSE-COLORED GLASSES

Of course it is natural to see certain people through rose-colored glasses, to think they are perfect, even though they aren't. Love, we know, is blind, and lovers commonly believe that the object of their affections can do no wrong. People often feel that way about authority figures, too—that they are flawless and cannot err.

Call it a process of self-deception if you like, but this push to perceive others as perfect is a wholly natural phenomenon. And, by and large, it is good and not bad—except that you have to realize what is going on and appreciate that people are not perfect even if we sometimes think they are.

Living with another person, for example, it is a blessing to be able to overlook their rough edges, and love helps with that.

It helps because people have a lot in common with cabinets and carpentry. In making a simple cabinet or in putting up a new wall, the end product will seem a lot prettier if the carpenter uses moldings to give it a finished look. They cover up the joints that don't really fit. People, too, need moldings, because few of us fit together perfectly. The rose-colored glasses that lovers wear work in much the same way.

Freud long ago pointed out that we idealize others. Children idealize their parents. Parents sometimes idealize their children. Many people idealize their leaders, and all this occurs naturally. It is one of God's ways of smoothing out human relations—to fit more moldings onto the rough edges of human life.

But these finishing touches are sometimes taken for the unalterable bottom-line truth. Don't be fooled. Enjoy the fantasy while it lasts, but don't mix it up with reality. For in reality, everyone is flawed, and at best there is only a birthmark on that otherwise dazzling cheek. The challenge of loving another person, then, cannot disregard imperfection. It must, instead, begin with a strategy to enable love in all of its forms to triumph in an imperfect world.

THE POWER OF LOVE

Loving another person when that person is never what he or she should be is possible, but not easy. It *is* possible, so rejoice in that. But beware, for much as guilt is oversold as a dangerous commodity, so is love oversold as the cure for all ills.

On the one hand, it is so, so good. The Baal Shem Tov, for example, founder of the pietistic Hasidic movement, explains the commandment "Love thy neighbor as thyself" in the following way: "It lies upon you to love your comrade as one like yourself. And who knows as you do your many defects? As you are nonetheless able to love yourself, so love your fellow no matter how many defects you may see in him."

Love is, according to the Baal Shem Tov, a transforming emotion, freely offered in spite of whatever defects it finds. It is a tremendous resource and can be called up in order to overcome the bad feelings that human vices have created.

Love offered for free is the emotional source for forgiveness. When two siblings have fought for years, they are likely to have created high-interest bank accounts where their anger grows even though no new deposits are made. The anger accumulates and compounds. It takes on a life all of its own.

How do you close the account? Love is the best way. A decision to let bygones be bygones. Lifting up the telephone, calling and saying, I really love you, let us begin again. That is the best way. Nothing works like love.

Nevertheless, the case for love cannot be so simply made. After all, do you think that belief in the power of love should be so very great that you ought to marry a cad and a well-known wife beater because you will be able to overcome his defects with the power and purity of your love? Live with him for a while—and one of you will be filled with guilt. Overlook the facts of a sordid past because of love? Or in the name of love should you be prepared to forgive a killer, even a mass killer who is guilty of killing millions of people because it is better to love and forgive than to be forever alienated from a fellow human being?

Or what of the simpler case: the man who has been so close

to his wife and has built a life together with her. She is extraordinary and he is extraordinary, too. But he, as is the way with men in their forties and their fifties, wants to test the waters to be sure that he is still very much alive. And he comes back and tells his wife that he doesn't love her any more even though he has a deep personal respect for her. He says to her: Forgive me. I have found a true love with whom I want to live the rest of my life. Let us now be friends.

And she? More often than not she is left high and dry, with three kids and with dreams of getting old with this man that will come to nought. Should she make him feel guilty or forgive him as he asks?

The power of human love to sweeten relationships that have gone sour is a great power indeed. But there are two kinds of love, and that means that there are two ways that love can help make it possible to accept another, blemishes and all.

TWO KINDS OF LOVE

First, there is *unconditional love.* In the old psychology books, that love was always associated with mothers. But fathers, too, have equal access to such love. Unconditional love presupposes that you *do not have to be worthy* to be loved. That you exist, and that you are who you are, is enough. As Erich Fromm puts it: "Mother loves the newborn infant because it is her child, not because the child has fulfilled any specific condition, or lived up to any specific expectation."[1]

Then there is *conditional love:* "Granted on condition that . . ." It is a love that has to be merited in order to be obtained.

Of the two, *unconditional love* is normally thought of as the more pious of the two. That is the love referred to by the Baal Shem Tov. It is nonjudgmental, for be a person good or bad, you will still love him. And you will forgive him for whatever he does. You will forgive all the rough places and you will smooth them out with the balm of your love. And such love has great power.

Conditional love, on the other hand, requires the recipient to merit the love. Take that woman with the three kids whose husband has just left her for a young flame. He says: I don't want to hurt you, forgive me, and let's be friends. And she feels angry. Who is right, and what should she do?

Simple: berate him, punish him, and make his life miserable. Because that is what he deserves.

Two people who live together and love together are held together by more than unconditional love. Their marriage created a unit that in all likelihood had its start with intense and inexplicable feelings of love. But as soon as they loved each other, they obligated each other as well. The bonds they consecrated when they made a marriage contract formalized the ties of emotion and obligation which are the package in which such love can be delivered day in and day out. They depended upon each other. There were unwritten assurances of welcome and of exclusivity that protected their love. And an "affair" is not just a good time. It is a bomb that destroys the expectations and obligations that were generated by "conditional" love. When the conditions are not kept, then the building starts to fall. How should a person feel when betrayed? Mad, blazing mad.

And what should happen as a result? The betrayer should be made to feel lousy, that is what. Forget the seamy sweetness he wants from his wife. She should forgive him? Forget it! She should let him stew.

Do you find this a surprising and a heartless idea? It may very well be, but it is the consequence of moral turpitude. It is a consequence of assuming that people should act responsibly, and that they should pay the costs of the damage they inflict. Here is a husband who doesn't feel guilty. He doesn't want to feel guilty. That is why he wants to patch everything up with a Band-Aid of love. But the truth is that love is now a piece of the artillery he uses to perpetrate his wrong.

THE ROMANCE OF GOD AND MAN

The romance of human loving is a romance made up of both unconditional and conditional love. Because they are often difficult to separate out, perhaps it would be helpful to see an extraordinary paradigm of this love, the Biblical love of God and man.

God chooses the People of Israel. That is a romance that begins for no reason that is apparent. Because God loves Israel, He gets involved with her.

Just think about it. He doesn't have to. The God of Aristotle, for example, was a God who deigned to contemplate a perfect object. Since there is only one perfect object, and that is God, Aristotle's God ended up contemplating Himself. The God of the Bible, on the other hand, decides, for better or worse, for richer or poorer, to throw in His lot with an imperfect object— with the people of Israel.

And it is exactly because He is God and because, therefore, He doesn't have to love anybody else, that His love is so important and palpable. It is a grand romance. When the prophet Jeremiah pictures God looking back on this romance He, God, thinks of it in terms of the romance of their youth. "I remember for thee the affection of thy youth, the love of thine espousals; how thou wentest after Me in the wilderness, in a land that was not sown" (Jeremiah 2:2).

UNCONDITIONAL LOVE

But some romance it was. Do you remember the story of the exodus and the events that follow soon thereafter? The stubbornness of the people and God's constant frustration with them? Nevertheless, it is love. And it is a love that comes to have its rules, its ideals, its expectations. And if those are cast away, if waywardness and sin take the place of commitment and purity, then God is filled with anger, and the relationship is stormy, to say the least. All because there are *expectations* in this love. And if they are disappointed, then the love too is a disappointing love.

Isaiah, Jeremiah, Amos, Hosea, all the prophets sing a chorus to this song of love. But it is a chorus filled with chastisements. Because, though it begins unconditionally, it is also a conditional love. And yet God holds out the prospect of a time of forgiveness—when the people will repent, and when he will take them back.

Because there are two sides to love, two kinds of love. Unconditional love creates a relationship, is one of the products of the relationship, and can often reestablish it when it has gone bad. Conditional love is one of the products of that relationship because relations have dimensions of responsibility, and they cause guilt when they are abused.

To love someone, then, who is never what he or she should be requires two things: recovering, where possible, the unconditional love that brought the two together. And creating the conditions to solve the problems generated by betraying conditional love.

How is this achieved?

REPENT, AGAIN, BEFORE IT IS TOO LATE

Through the way of repentance.

Remorse. Expect to feel bad if your love for someone else has been seriously hurt. It is not at all the case that being in love means that you never have to say that you are sorry, as Erich Segal's *Love Story* claimed several years ago. Being in love is part of being ready *to say you are sorry.* There are few phrases that are quite so full of love as "I am sorry." And such words simply express the feelings that lie underneath: a person hurts.

Husbands and wives must realize that marriage will inevitably entail feeling bad. It may be blissful, but it is not only bliss. Because so many people assume that if they feel angry and bad they must not be in love, they will decide that the path of virtue is to deny feeling bad. That anger is considered irreverent and dangerous. It is denied or suppressed, sublimated rather than recognized.

And what happens as a result? The fire of love is put out. In the language so often used today, the electricity is turned off. The feelings seem gone.

But remorse, bad feelings, are a natural response to doing wrong. Mind you, it is not always clear who has done wrong. Someone may be angry because he or she feels guilty. Someone else may be angry because he or she has been wronged. There are many possibilities. But the bottom line is simply this: two people don't stick together like glue. They glide in and out over a small distance, and the tracks they are on need to be constantly repaired. Yes, the molding of love may make it seem as if the two sides of the joint are always perfect. But the tensions in the joint are well known to the people alternately coming together and pulling apart.

Recognize your bad feelings. In tough straits, no one will be willing to work hard enough if it doesn't seem like there is something to fix. The general rule, "Don't fix it if it ain't broke," is a rule we usually follow in love. But don't wait until it is so broke that it can't be fixed before you say, "Now let's give it a try."

Remorse is followed by:

Recantation or confession. Talk about how you feel. You can spend hours, days, and years analyzing yourself and your mate. You can have that other person all figured out. But why don't you invest a little bit of energy in telling that other one what you think, what is on your mind?

Sure, you must beware when you speak so intimately. How many people use their introspective analyses of someone else in order to throw sophisticated darts? But whether the darts are finely crafted or whether they are crudely hewn, darts they are nonetheless.

People will sometimes use guilt instead of anger as a more acceptable dart. It is, after all, a more acceptable emotion. Instead of attacking others with obvious venom, we tell them they have failed us. We have succeeded in making them feel bad, which is our real purpose, and in addition we have placed ourselves in the morally virtuous position. And we do not seem like the kind of crass people who get angry.[2]

That is the caveat about "talking it out." Don't be cruel. Don't expect everything to be solved by talking. But don't stop talking because it cannot solve all the problems. Talk, talk, and talk some more. When you get home from work, talk. Don't wait for a big occasion. Don't allow everything to collect until the dam breaks. Talk, talk, talk. Talk about the things that matter to you. Talk about the things that you think you should maybe talk about. Take cues from each other to be able to respect those (probably) few areas where you don't have to let it all hang out. Sure, we have to put up with a few things we don't like, and it doesn't make any sense to keep complaining about them all the time.

But there are so many problems that can be solved if there is an honest give and take that is as much a part of two people's lives as paying the bills or getting up and going to work.

Does this mean that we always have to shout it out? Not at all. What this means is that it is possible to talk to someone else respectfully about the things that matter to you. If you do, then it is very likely that the other one will be so impressed that both of you will be able to talk with each other.

Indeed this is not like confessing to God. No one is God, and there are private places that people have that they should not feel obligated to reveal. But the general principle still holds. What happens when an emotion makes it to the level of the lips is usually a positive experience, and one that makes change possible.

Either the emotion itself, once brought to the surface, makes certain actions possible which heretofore were not, or the emotion, once brought to the surface, becomes subject to rational control. Either possibility offers a new opportunity, and movement can begin to take place.

Renunciation. If you are the guilty party, renounce your wrongdoing and decide not to commit it again. If the other party is guilty, try to make that clear, not with a hammer, but with a prism that helps to refract a complex light. Through the medium of language, which expresses feelings, see whether you can arrive at a point where the other feels remorse, says it, and renounces the wrongdoing.

Resolution. Don't be caught up in the past. Look toward a shared future which is yours, closer together. Plan changes in your routine which will make it less likely for problems to recur. Resolve to talk more often. To be less . . . To be more . . . Make a concrete plan, a resolution, and try to achieve it. Not wishful thinking, but resolution. If you were asked to achieve a new level of sales in your management position, you wouldn't get away with simply wishing for those sales, would you? You will never work out your problems with your husband or wife if you arrive at the stage only of wishing for an improvement. Sell the solution to yourselves, and carry it out.

Don't be caught up in the past. Don't focus only on the problems, on the defects and the blemishes. It is reported of Rabbi Zusya, the great ecstatic, that even when someone did evil in his presence he saw in him only good. According to legend, he reached this stage because once after he had embarrassed a sinner, his teacher blessed him to see only the good in other people.[3]

See the good in your wife. See the good in your husband. See the good in your children. See the good in your secretary. See the good in your parents, who are fallible but probably also very good. Look for the good. It helps when searching for the balance we need to be able to tolerate that which is bad.

Finally, *reconciliation*, the culminating repentant act.

UNTIL YOUR NEIGHBOR IS APPEASED

According to the Talmud, and to all later codes of Jewish law, religion has its limits, and God will not forgive all sins. On the Day of Atonement, for example, repentance and the rituals of the day are said to secure forgiveness only for transgressions committed against God. Which, we ought to remember, are many but not enough to empty the ample stores of transgression we keep.

God will not forgive transgressions against another person—will not, at least, until that other person has been appeased. *You have to ask someone else to forgive you before God will step in.*[4] Before going to the synagogue on the sacred Day of Atonement, we are required to go to each other and to say: Will you forgive me for the transgressions I have committed against you during the last year?

An awesome two words: Forgive me.

As always, beseeching forgiveness is humbling and somewhat debasing. When truly meant, such a request is very moving to speak and very moving to hear. It involves bowing down low. Thus it is that Moses, the humble, "bowed himself down to the 'level of the ground' and love for one another then entered the heart of all who saw and heard."

Forgiveness involves restitution. If you have injured someone, physically, emotionally, or by having harmed his or her property, you must provide the proper restitution first. And then, partly by virtue of the restitution you have given, and partly by virtue of the intent which such restitution manifests, you must ask for forgiveness. Even if you have angered someone, you can not let it pass by. Anger is a form of personal injury, and every effort must be taken to appease the person whom you have hurt, to undo the wrong to the extent that it can be undone, in order for atonement to be made.

Nan Robertson, in her book *Getting Better: Inside Alcoholics Anonymous*, describes the necessary repentant steps that alcoholics must take in order to change their own behavior. Among them is making amends to those we have harmed. There is great renewal and great love generated by such amends. Without that step, reconciliation cannot adequately take place.[5]

And the person who is asked for his forgiveness is required to give it.

Here again, the normal caveats once again hold. Everyone must be sincere. The forms themselves have little meaning if they do not lead to both a change of heart and a change of deed.

A battered wife, for example, tells of her own plight and that of many other women who are skewered on the rod of forgiveness. "Most important," she writes, "in between the batterings, he sincerely repents. He begs forgiveness and promises, 'It will never happen again.' He also threatens, 'If you tell anyone what I did, you will pay for it.' I was continuously assured that it had stopped, that the nightmare was over. I believed it—until the next incident."[6]

A change of heart, and a change of deed.

Of course, there are apologies that grease the wheels of social life. But they are more a matter of form than function. The Japanese make many apologies: when entering a room, for example, they say they are making a nuisance of themselves. And they apologize similarly when they leave. A polite Japanese expresses contrition when serving a dinner to a house guest, saying "I don't think this will suit your taste." Appearances are what count. The apologies assure social harmony, but have little to do with questions of right and wrong.[7]

Asking forgiveness involves a reorientation of perspective. Instead of one person standing above the other, effectively bowing down low enables two people to stand side by side.

Interestingly, such an effect can sometimes be achieved in odd ways. In some cases, for example, children live with the burden of having surpassed their parents' material accomplishments. Many women will feel guilty about wearing a fur coat while their mothers, products of a more frugal and materially lacking generation, still wear cloth. Wearing the fur would tend to put the child higher than the parent. Therefore she feels guilty.

How to handle it? Put the parent up high. Buy her one, too, and a better one than you would buy for yourself.

One man described how his father had been complaining loudly about him at family gatherings. He decided to take his father deep-sea fishing, an activity they had enjoyed when the son was a boy. "He renewed their relationship by doing that," says Dr. Ron Levant, the director of the Fatherhood Project at Boston University, where this man participated. "The father could again appropriately feel that he knew more than his son did. Each became more accepting of the other."

So keep in mind that we will never be able to live with one another if we expect perfection. We will never be worthy of each other if we do not try to achieve a more perfect love, as perfect as can be. To do so, we must be engaged in a lifelong effort to achieve reconciliation, through all the steps of repentance, and into that place which is the holy of holies to us, the heart of someone whom we love.

PART V
How Guilt Can Transform Society and Liberate Love

CHAPTER 17
Collective Guilt and Collective Repentance

*There is a collective guilt. . . . There is a
common responsibility for ensuring that
history does not repeat itself.*
—**West German Chancellor
Helmut Kohl**

*The new world must be built by resolute
men who when hope is dead will hope by
faith, who will neither seek premature
escape from the guilt of history, nor yet
call the evil, which taints all their
achievements, good.*
—**Reinhold Niebuhr**

Until this point in our book, we have focused on the guilt
that individuals feel, on the moral responsibility which such
guilt reveals and upon a variety of paths that lead from guilt
to reconciliation.

But the world is made up of more than individuals. Man is,
as Aristotle taught us, a social animal. He exists in families, in

communities, in nations. Does guilt follow him there? Is there another guilt, one that carries with it many of the same moral imperatives and perhaps even the same problems but which, however, is not the product so much of individual feelings as of feelings that are shared, not the product of an individual's conscience, but of a shared collective conscience?

The answer is important to know. We live in the post-Auschwitz era, and the legacy of such cataclysms in the civilized world is a moral burden that needs to be examined and reexamined day after day. In addition, compelling moral issues are raised continually in connection with collectivities: the responsibilities of corporations for protecting the environment, for example. Witness Union Carbide's debacle in Bhopal, and its efforts to assuage itself of guilt, or Exxon's contribution to the U.S. environment of a huge Alaskan oil spill, an event that "could not happen." These are but a few examples.

Statesman and political philosopher Edmund Burke has wisely observed that he did "not know the method of drawing up an indictment against an whole people."[1] Wisely, I say, because we cannot blame the innocent for wrongs they did not commit. Even so, shouldn't collectivities like corporations have a conscience? Don't nations bear the burdens of their past deeds? If so, then there must be another type of guilt, similar to individual guilt, but different in certain ways. It is collective guilt.

THE ARGUMENT AGAINST COLLECTIVE GUILT

There *is* collective guilt, though the concept is tempting to avoid. For several reasons:

First, in assessing the reasonableness of guilt, it is most important to establish a direct connection between cause and effect. You remember the example of a man who felt guilty for his mother's fall. We decided that he was plaguing himself with erroneous guilt. Neither his actions nor his inactions caused his mother's fall.

Can it possibly be said that young children, people who were not alive during the Holocaust, bear its guilt? They certainly do not bear any *personal* guilt. To say so would lessen the responsibility of those who were so clearly at fault.

This is a very good reason to be reticent about extending the concept of guilt. We run the risk of undermining the crucial importance of establishing a nexus between cause, effect, and ensuing guilt.

And there is a second reason to stay away from the notion of collective guilt—ironically, a particularly Jewish reason. For collective guilt is one of those weapons found in the arsenal of anti-Semitic ideas that has been used to mistreat and to destroy Jews and Jewish communities for eons. Jewish children in Poland, in Spain, in Argentina, and elsewhere have grown up having epithets hurled at them with rocks and with snowballs: "Christ-killers!" For Jews, it was claimed, bear collective guilt for the death of Jesus and therefore must suffer. Each year, while Christian communities prepared to celebrate the Passion of Jesus, Jewish communities cringed and suffered. Jews were beaten, pogroms were inflicted, all by virtue of the nefarious calumny that Jews, as a community, bore the burden of guilt for those who killed Jesus in ancient times. And that they deserved punishment for it.

Collective guilt rings such bells. And although the Vatican has clearly tried to put these ideas to rest in its important declaration *Nostre Aetate* which was adopted by the Second Vatican Council in 1965, it is hard to forget what they have meant in the past. So even while it may be tempting to raise the subject of collective guilt, I, for one, have to hold myself back from saying: "Never again!"

And yet, all this having been said, were we to ignore the way that guilt works in groups, the ways that corporations, communities, and nations examine their collective consciences, and the paths they take to amend their ways, then we would ignore a phenomenon which must be central to the moral well-being of our times.

WHAT IS COLLECTIVE GUILT?

Throughout the Bible, individuals sin. But from the Bible's perspective, something more is happening. Sin violates God's convenant with Israel, undermining the very foundation upon which the community's life is built. The prophets preached a sermon of doom, saying that the people's misdeeds, and especially the misdeeds of their leaders—the kings, nobles, priests, and false prophets—would lead surely to demise.[2]

Put simply, corrupt individuals and leaders destroy more than themselves; they tear apart the fabric that holds the society together. And for this reason the prayers of Jews to this day recount that the exile of Israel in ancient times was suffered "because of our sins." *Our* sins, please note, in the plural. Collective guilt.

Moreover, there is a collective *we* that speaks, acts, and sometimes suffers on our behalf. If someone is found slain in a field, the Bible says, and it is not known who has killed him, then the elders of the nearest city—acting on the population's behalf—feel a sense of responsibility. They symbolically slay a young heifer and wash their hands over this animal, saying "Our hands have not shed this blood, neither did our eyes see it done" (Deuteronomy 21:1–9).

Why the symbolic act? The Talmud suggests that perhaps the man had been hungry. When he came to the elders, they may have sent him away without food. The lack of food may have led to a lack of strength, and when it came time to defend himself against an assailant he could not. Or he might have found himself having to steal food from others, and as a result ended up getting himself killed. Other commentators say that the elders neglected to warn him and let him go into dangerous places without proper protection.[3]

The elders are the government. They fret about their responsibilities, whether they should have had a soup kitchen or not, and whether they are providing adequate police—concerns that should be theirs. And as a good government, they are worried that perhaps they are not doing a good job. Just think of the alternative: they could have paid no attention at

all! Instead, they have a guilty conscience, as they should—
on the people's behalf—when a homicide is found. Collective
guilt.

In more secular terms, collective guilt, much like individual
guilt, is the product of violating moral codes. As individuals
violate those codes, so do collectivities of individuals. A corporation, for example, operates on two levels. Its individuals act,
and sometimes they may act unethically and incur guilt as a
result—like a stockbroker violating securities laws and becoming liable to prosecution because of his individual wrongs.

But corporations act as entities, too, and a corporation can be
justly charged with negligent behavior, with violating securities
laws, with not taking a community's safety into account with
respect to the disposal of harmful chemicals, or for intentionally
overcharging the government hundreds of dollars for a simple
widget that costs a few cents.

Now it is important to know who is responsible, because it
may be important to know who is liable and who can therefore
be punished. Take the 1989 Exxon oil spill in Alaska, for example. While all the facts are not yet in, there appears to have been
a drunk captain, and he was certainly not acting responsibly.
But even though his actions (or inactions) were an immediate
cause of the problem, should he be the only one who incurs
guilt? Obviously not. There are others who were involved: the
management personnel responsible for seeing that the captains
are doing their jobs, or those responsible for not having a clean-
up crew constantly on call, as was earlier proposed by environ-
mentalists. But is that the end? Should these few individuals be
held liable for a massive and costly oil spill?

Again, no. They were acting as agents for a corporation. Although it may be possible to hold them liable for specific actions, at the same time the corporation is an active entity. It is
the corporation that had the resources to be in the position of
transporting huge amounts of oil, and the corporation that
bears the major brunt of the responsibility for the disaster that
took place.

There is more than a simple chain of cause and effect that
operates here. Where a collectivity is involved, there may be a

"responsible party" who is not a person but rather a collectivity of persons.

The same can be said for soldiers who may commit immoral acts when in battle. If they individually slay innocent people as was sometimes the case during the Vietnam War, then they must be prosecuted for having committed murder. But entire armies could conceivably be, and in fact have been, committed to carrying out immoral policies. Then a larger entity is responsible.

If we take the Nazi government during World War II as an example, we see that the institutions of government were used to create the machinery and to execute the plans for killing millions of people because they were Jews, or because they were members of other ethnic or ideological groups. The governments are then guilty.

But who is the government? Its top leadership? All its policy-makers? Those who carried out the policies? And why shield others? What about those who stood by knowing that a policy was immoral but who felt that their inaction shielded them from moral responsibility? The philosophers of the culture who created its underlying values? The public relations people and the teachers who disseminated those values? Who is responsible? All of the above?

You see, then, that the cause and effect relationships in a community's life are highly complex. To say, however, that they do not exist, or that the product of their existence is something that bears no moral responsibility is to hide, I think, from the realities that in fact have created the most devastating events of history.

Add to this another reality of corporate or communal life, that collectivities have life spans different from those of individuals. Sometimes they are shorter. Very often, especially in the case of nations, they are far longer. When individuals die, their personal moral responsibility dies with them. At best, their deaths are an atonement for their sins.

But corporations exist whether their chief operating officers are here today or gone tomorrow. And nations and national groups continue to exist after the major players on today's stage are only a vague memory. All these communal entities carry their pasts with them and the responsibilities accrued by the deeds of the past. They also carry with them the baggage of their collective memories by which their own stories become woven into a larger story which at some point is called history.

CULTURE AND ITS OBLIGATIONS

The facts of history provide a vantage point for learning about the collective personality of a culture. This personality is the product of the poets and their sagas, of the artists and their visions. It is also the product of the craftsmen and the business-men of the past, and those who have created the state. In profound ways, from the vocabulary we use to communicate with each other to the economic well-being of our society, we in the present are all the beneficiaries of the past.

And every society has a collective memory, the sum total of its past experiences. Beyond that, its moral life is a complex reality made up of responses to the deeds of the past, responses which, one hopes, appropriate the good of generations gone by and transform past evils to make life better than it was.

Consider American society and its many social problems. Any analysis of today's inner-city problems and the economic dimensions of a chronically unemployed underclass, must make reference to the legacy of slavery which is still with us— not because we have slaves today, but because we have still not figured out how to fully integrate all black citizens into the communal fabric of our great and wealthy democracy. We have made extraordinary strides, no doubt. But so much is still left to be done.

In solely American terms, then, our society continues to bear the burden of slavery. We have "collective guilt" which should be gnawing at us every day.

Personally, I had nothing to do with American slavery. My own ancestors did not even arrive on these shores until well after the Civil War. And yet it is my problem, too, my problem as a member of a collectivity, my country, of which I hope to be a morally responsible part. I receive my country's gifts, which are so many, even though I did nothing to deserve them. And I receive its burdens, even though I did nothing to deserve them, either.

When I see someone in the subway or on the street who has no home, the problem is not whether I have caused the problem —I haven't—nor even what I do then and there to relieve the problem—whether I give this poor person a handout or not. The greater issue is: What can be done to remove the problem, to care for those who cannot be responsible for themselves, and to make training, jobs, and housing available to those who can? How can I help to feed the needy? I then have to ask myself: How do I as an individual contribute to my society's ability to repent its past sins and to be good? Through my government? Through my business? Through my charity? Through my own work?

History and collective memory provide problems that become my own, and if this is true in terms of the problems we inherit in a democratic society which is relatively just, how much more disturbing and complex are the problems which are the burdens of societies that are patently unjust.

GERMANY AND THE HOLOCAUST

The most important example of collective guilt is the problem faced by modern-day Germany and the guilt that German society bears with it for the Holocaust.

There are, first, those still alive who served in the SS or in the German army. As well, there are those Germans and other collaborators who are still alive and who stood by silently during the war as Jews were rounded up and shipped away.

As Richard von Weizsaecker, President of the Federal Republic of Germany, has noted:

> . . . Too many people . . . tried not to notice what was happening. There were many ways of not burdening one's conscience, of shunning responsibility, looking the other way, keeping silent.

Their guilt and their shame cannot be forgotten.

But today's German youth bear a different burden. They have to live with the memory that their own parents or grandparents played a part, that they or their close friends may be living in apartments taken from others who were sent to their deaths, that their education may have been paid for by the gold stolen from the victims, that their economy as it is today is filled with corporations that are alive and well and that were themselves the beneficiaries of slave labor in the recent past.[4] Should any of these corporations help other nations to produce poison gas, as was the case during 1989, then it is today's German citizens that will have to remember that their scientists and their corporations produced the Xyklon-B that was used to gas millions of people in gas chambers which were made to look like simple showers. The young generation has to live with this, to learn from it, and to act responsibly in light of its own nation's peculiar and distressing past. Theirs is an enormous burden, for they live with a collective guilt that few nations have to bear.

And the story neither begins nor ends with Germany. How many historical blank spots still remain to be filled in? When will we see a full accounting for Stalin's crimes, and for those of Mao Tse-tung? When will we be able to understand the moral dimensions of Pol Pot's devastation of Cambodia? Of who did what and why there was an insufficient international response? Many more are the ghosts in the closets of the modern world.

The rendering of accounts that individuals do from time to time is a rendering they need for themselves in order to position themselves so that they can change their lives.

Will communities do the same? Will we finally call them to account for their deeds? Perhaps then the very process of history will become a process which allows for atonement and repentance at the corporate level of life.

For as there is collective guilt, there is collective repentance as well.

COLLECTIVE REPENTANCE

Whether it be a corporation, a nation, or even, were it conceivable, all of mankind, there are paths, a wide variety of forms, rituals, symbols, and transforming activities that make up what Rabbi Abraham Isaac Hacohen Kook, Israel's first chief rabbi, calls "general penitence." General penitence, he says, involves all cultural forms through which the world rises from decadence to an improvement of the social and economic order.[5]

Man cannot repent only for himself. He repents for his community, too. In all the prayers which are publicly offered for forgiveness on Yom Kippur, the plural is used. On the one hand, that is a way of saying that even if we did not commit a sin personally, someone in the community surely has. But beyond that, the community prays as a unit. Individuals have their responsibilities toward God. But so do communities. And the community, in toto, must ask forgiveness for its sins. Thus Maimonides says:

> It is necessary therefore that everyone, throughout the year, should regard himself as if he were half innocent and half guilty, and should regard the whole of mankind as half innocent and half guilty. If then he commits one more sin, he presses down the scale of guilt against himself and the whole world and causes his destruction. If he fulfills one commandment, he turns the scale of merit in his favor and in that of the whole world and brings salvation and deliverance to all his fellow-creatures and to himself, as it is said, "The righteous man is the foundation of the world" (Proverbs 10:25); this is to say, that he who acts justly presses down the scale of merit in favor of all the world and saves it.[6]

From the individual to mankind is a small step to take—a small step since the human spirit manifests itself not only in the lives of individuals, but in the life of human communities. And the transformation of the human community occurs in ways not unlike the transformation of the single human self. It involves remorse, recantation, renunciation, resolution, and reconciliation.

Collective repentance is the renewal of the world's spirit. It is the lifting up of that spirit, the recovery of the divine, the bringing on of spring after the winters of our life. History yearns for penitential acts much the way that seedlings try so hard to break forth from the ground every year. The energies of man, therefore, have to be placed in this direction, too. Not only to bring economic miracles, but to bring a true renewal of spirit, a renewal that cannot take place without repentance first.

FORGIVENESS FOR THE HOLOCAUST

But is repentance possible where it is most necessary? The killing of six million Jews, over a million of them innocent children, and of five million others in cold blood, presents the greatest challenge to ethics. The Holocaust gives new meaning to evil; it easily undermines our confidence in man and in progress. It wearies, perhaps forever, the world's spirit.

Yet, does it leave room for penitential acts? Are there ways to atone for so many millions of deaths? Can they, should they, be forgiven, in order to allow mankind to liberate itself from such horror? Or must they never be forgiven to make sure that such events as the horror of Sonderkommandos taking whole towns out to the field, having them dig ditches, and then shooting all the people dead, or of gassing millions and burning their bodies in furnaces will still be able to sear the consciousness of young boys and girls who are still children today or who are to be born tomorrow?

Years ago, my teacher Professor Abraham Joshua Heschel was asked basically the same question. He had been invited to a retreat by one of America's largest corporations for its executive personnel. Professor Heschel had lectured on the importance of compassion and understanding, and had covered, as part of his material, the necessity for people to forgive others for their shortcomings. As a result of his presentation, one of the leaders of the company challenged the professor to forgive the Germans for the Holocaust. Professor Heschel answered by telling a story about one of the great rabbinic personalities of the last century, Rabbi Hayyim Brisker (Brisker meaning "from the town of Brisk").

Rabbi Hayyim was a widely respected and famous rabbi in his day. Once, he visited a distant community and was returning home to Brisk by train. As was common in those days, he rode in a compartment with others. His travel mates were rich men, returning from the country after having completed a major business deal.

Now it was Rabbi Hayyim's personal custom to dress and to act simply. In fact, he could not be distinguished from any poor, common man. In the compartment of the train, the rich men celebrated their success, eating and drinking, but failing, significantly, to offer the distinguished rabbi who looked like a poor hungry man even a morsel of food.

When the train finally arrived in Brisk, the rich men immediately noticed that crowds of people were waiting at the station, and they surmised that some famous man must have been on board the train. When they alighted from their car, they saw that the crowd surged forward toward them and that it was the poor man in their compartment who was the object of the crowd's adulation. Rabbi Hayyim was carried on the shoulders of his followers, and he addressed them shortly with words of greeting.

The rich men were aghast. They realized immediately that they had failed to treat their fellow traveler decently and they sought out the rabbi to ask his forgiveness. "I will not forgive you," said Rabbi Hayyim. They were horrified. They reminded the rabbi of what he certainly knew, that according to Jewish law, a man who begs for forgiveness must be forgiven. Could it be that the great Rabbi Hayyim did not remember so fundamental a law?

Rabbi Hayyim responded once again, "I do not forgive you." But this time he went on to explain just why. "It is not for me to forgive you," said Rabbi Hayyim. "You did not offend *me*. Had you known who I was, you would have been more than ready to treat me with dignity and you would never have acted offensively to me. You did not therefore wrong me. You wronged all the poor people in the city of Brisk and everywhere else in the world. You must ask for forgiveness from them."

Professor Heschel then went on: "During the Holocaust, I was a professor in Cincinnati, sitting in a soft and comfortable chair while millions of people were gassed and burned. Why do you ask me to forgive the killers? Go to victims. Ask them."

Professor Heschel's story must be the starting point. The victims themselves are gone. It is they who must truly be asked to forgive. But that is, of course, one of the great tragedies of murder, that the victim cannot forgive. There is no reconciliation that is possible where that reconciliation must first take place.

Yet there is more to be said. Though beseeching forgiveness is so fundamental to the process of repentance, there are other paths, too—paths that are important to take—especially where a great calamity cannot and should not be erased.

Guarantee accountability. Open up records, such as those held by the United Nations, which can be helpful in prosecuting those who have done wrong. And be sure that the guilty are punished for their deeds—even at this late date. For if people get away with their crimes, what does it say about the collective morality of society? As much as the crimes themselves undermined morality by making the unthinkable possible, morality is further undermined if there is no accountability.

Make reparations. Continue to create special bonds of friendship that reach across the abyss, bonds from Germany to Israel, the uniquely Jewish nation that came into being after the Holocaust.

Teach the history of the Holocaust. Tell the story of the innocent children and their parents, how they suffered though they did no wrong; tell this far and wide, so that it will enter into mankind's collective memory. So that all over, all people will say: Our image is diminished, too, and our conscience hurts, for we, too, are human beings, and perhaps we, too, could do that. Sharing the shame is one of the ways that the guilt itself, once collectively felt, will help to redeem mankind.

And the story of the Holocaust must be told in detail, in terms of Hitler's war against the Jews—not only as a general comment on evil, but as a specific example of the evil of anti-Semitism. For unless that is understood, the reality of the destruction, as well as the reality of Jewish renewal in the modern age—the founding of Israel and its ongoing preservation and development—will not be properly understood.

My people have suffered unspeakably and returned to life. Not easily, and not certainly. What is so precious to me, and what is so central to my cares will, I hope, be understood by all those who can, I believe, empathize with our destruction and renewal. We are all renewed when we take an active part in an injured people's rebirth.

CAN A FLOWER YET BLOOM?

"Penitence is inspired by the yearning of all existence to be better, purer, more vigorous and on a higher plane than it is," says Rabbi Kook.[7] He calls for "a bud to come forth," which will manifest that penitence. It is heartening to see such buds.

On August 12, 1985, five hundred and twenty people died in the crash of a Japan Air Lines plane, the world's worst single plane disaster. Two months later, the president of Japan Air Lines faced the relatives of the victims and bowed low and long. After turning to a wall covered with wooden tablets bearing the victim's names, he bowed again. And in a voice that sometimes quavered, Yasumoto Takagi asked for forgiveness and accepted responsibility.[8]

One by one, people walked up to the altar, left a chrysanthemum for remembrance, bowed and turned away. Families, dignitaries, and airline employees walked up to the altar for more than an hour, pausing to pray, wipe away a tear, or stand silently.

For Japan Air Lines, this service marked the culmination of a two-month exercise in accountability. In the days right after the accident, when family members traveled to a small mountain village to identify the bodies, airline staff stayed with them, paying all expenses, bringing them food, drink, and clean clothes. Staff people stayed with the families to arrange for funerals or to block intrusive reporters. Japan Air Lines set up scholarship funds for children whose parents died. It spent $1.5 million on two elaborate memorial services. Executives attended every victim's funeral, although some were turned away. The airlines will split compensation payments with the Boeing company that will probably exceed $100 million.

The airline felt it had to perform these acts of conciliation, for otherwise it would have been accused of inhumanity and irresponsibility. Naturally, the airline's self-interest was at stake. Its quick admission of responsibility and its personal help to family members created a web of gratitude and obligation that discouraged legal remedies. A cumbersome legal system in Japan also made families reluctant to sue. But how striking it is to see a corporation bowing down low, occupied with forms of penance. It is not hard to imagine that the entire experience could have been nothing more or less than a courtroom drama, the bereaved families fighting for a lucrative settlement, the airline saying: We will give you less.

The world longs for atoning acts: for corporations whose boards of directors and whose executive leadership will have the courage to apologize and to make amends; for political leaders who will feel accountable to their people and to the history of their nations.

It longs for the courageous stands and actions which defend human liberty and dignity. It longs for righteousness in the arena of nations. Human society needs to be reminded that all groups bear responsibility, and that historical wrongs can be righted. And each of us carries, therefore, on his shoulders, some of the burden of our wronged fellow human beings. So that each of us then can have a part in the redemption the world needs.

CHAPTER 18

Purity

Idolatry is the root source of our sin and wrongdoing. Ultimately, all idolatry is worship of the self, projected and objectified. . . . In proclaiming as ultimate the ideas and programs to which we are devoted, we are but proclaiming the work of our minds to be the final truth of life. In the last analysis, the choice is only between love of God and love of self, between a God-centered and self-centered existence.
—**Will Herberg,**
Judaism and Modern Man

Only humble men who recognize the mystery and the majesty are able to face both the beauty and terror of life without exulting over its beauty or becoming crushed by its terror.
—**Reinhold Niebuhr**

We are drawing near to the end of this climb. It has led us from the self to others, and then beyond, to the larger communities in which we live. Everywhere along the way, the route that has been chosen has been in response to guilt feelings and to a guilty conscience, which by and large I have praised rather than condemned.

To where, though, does this lead? Can we say that it leads to a loftier sense of the self and be satisfied with that? Can we say that it leads to a finer sense of community and be satisfied with that? We might be so satisfied, but then the task would still be incomplete.

The goal of guilt is purity before God. The yearning for perfection which gives rise to guilt in the first place is a yearning for spiritual purity, a yearning for closeness to God. It is a yearning for a joyful feeling, a joyful feeling of being accepted by and challenged by God; a joyful feeling that comes from recognizing that it is good to be a human creature, forever imperfect and forever wanting to be more.

PURIFYING THE UPROOTED AND IMPURE

How does this work? How can we mortals come to understand better God's purifying power so that we can search for and find it? God's purifying touch may not be fully understandable, but it is not beyond comprehension.

The Talmud devotes one of its sections to a discussion of offerings that were required by Scripture to be given to the priests.[1] The agricultural produce of the land was tithed, and a portion of these tithes was set apart for the priests. This special portion of the harvest had to be kept in a special state of purity, free from all contact with death, for it would ultimately be eaten by the priests within the temple precincts, where only complete ritual purity was permitted.

What then if these plants would, in the meantime, become exposed to one of a number of factors that would render them ritually impure? Could they still be given to the priests to be eaten in the temple? They could not, unless they were replanted in the ground. By being replanted, they were considered no longer in the class of food; by being replanted, they became plants that were growing again, and they no longer carried impurity.

I am fascinated by the laws of the plucked-up plants, because the same is true for human beings. Each of us is uprooted. Each of us feels a sense of anomie, of separateness from our source. And when we are so separate, contact with the impure makes us impure.

What is it like to be so unattached? Paul Tillich says it nicely: people are "estranged from the ultimate power of being," submerged in anxiety, loneliness and guilt, disillusioned by always collapsing "idolatries" of nationalism, technology, possessions, sex, or success. Sin, he says, is "separation"—separation from others, from one's self, from the "Ground" of one's being. "We not only suffer . . . because of the self-destructive consequences of our separation, but also know why we suffer," Tillich says. "We know that we are estranged from something to which we really belong. . . ."

We are plucked up out of the "Ground."

The classic existentialist writers capture this feeling again and again. Modern man is uprooted, cut off from feelings and from the sources of his own existence, plagued with the trivia of life, captured by the meaninglessness of his own existence.

Do you remember the beginning of Albert Camus's book *The Stranger*? *"Aujourd'hui, maman est morte."* "Mother died today. Or, maybe, yesterday; I can't be sure."

An event of great significance is reduced to another meaningless act. Camus describes how the protagonist's mother died in a home and how he seldom saw her during her last year. He glosses over any guilt he might feel and concentrates rather on what it would have meant to lose his Sunday, not to mention the bother of going to the bus, getting his ticket, and spending two hours each way on the journey.

These are the complaints that I hear from people every day: that the trivial tasks of life have come to overtake the grounded concerns that really purify.

An unattached human being lacks roots for his spirit. He has no cause, no focus, for his life other than what he decides for the moment to commit himself to.

Most people do, in fact, try to attach themselves to some ground. It prevents them from having no place at all. For many, work provides that center of attachment. For others, it is a cause to which they give their lives. But for most rootless people, the prevailing winds take them like tumbleweeds wherever the breezes will go. They must throw their lives into the fad of the moment, the music of the moment, today's cult or tomorrow's technology, so that they can have it all and seek, by having so much, to strike a root that will possibly keep them from blowing away. And yet the winds of time will blow them tomorrow just as they were blown today. For they have not struck any roots in a soil that will really hold.

Is there a human being who does not, at some time, feel the need to search? To search for the great mysteries that ask the deepest questions about our existence? To be drawn deeply into those mysteries, into the shadows that, while somewhat frightening, still offer the sense that here, yes, here, the search is really worthwhile.

Culture leads us toward many paths that strike a chord of certainty, chords that sound to say that the mystery has meaning. So many of us are drawn toward music, toward art, toward literature, because we sense intuitively that here there is a true ground. People who walk without any thought of religion also know that a secular sense of ethics can take them there. That in an "ethical culture" they will be finally applying their lives to tasks that are worthy of human beings.

That is why guilt is so extraordinary a starting point. Why guilt, with its intellectual complexities, draws us in further to a sense that we are walking, at last, in a land that has in it a bush that burns and that is not consumed. Guilt has led us here, searching for a rootedness for ethics—a search that ends by joining other searches which look, ultimately, for the true and the last Ground in which we can plant ourselves and our transient lives.

MAN IS VULNERABLE

Transience so marks man because each human being is a vulnerable creature. He is physically vulnerable. His body can hurt so much as it becomes sick and withers. And he is morally vulnerable, having feelings and a conscience that can hurt.

Few of us are unaware of our physical vulnerability. Sooner

or later, the teenager who knows that he will live forever learns that life is much shorter and much more tenuous than that. When friends die, when loved ones pass on, the sense of physical weakness which we share with one another is a sense that becomes clear to us all, and, I would add, a great source of empathy.

Guilt is a signpost of that vulnerability, and it is placed on other vaults that hide the mysteries of human life. The guilt, for example, that survivors feel. Soldiers see their friends die in the line of battle and often find that their own lives become troublesome sources of guilt. Survivors of the Holocaust—like Primo Levi, who committed suicide, filled with guilt for being alive—find themselves guilty for living while others do not. Guilt is, for them, not simply a solution for wrongs done. Guilt is a signpost that reminds them—as it should remind every human being—of the troublesome wonder of our existence, an existence that is normally a source of joy, but an existence that is occasionally a source of pain and heartache due to its vulnerability.

Elaine Pagels has observed that guilt is, itself, a way of overcoming vulnerability. Human beings are subject to so many onslaughts like sickness and death that fear easily overcomes us. It is, she says, satisfying to feel that we have brought so much pain upon ourselves. That is why religion so often is comfortable with such ideas. For they are better than the alternative: that life is chaos, and that we lack control.[2]

But we are also *morally* vulnerable. To be human is to sin, and to feel bad about it. And to be human is to empathize with someone else, to ask yourself: What would I have done were I there? Think of that in terms of the Holocaust: Not just "How could they have stood by?" but even more: "Will I stand by the next time someone is persecuted, when peoples are destroyed, when violence seizes the reigns of power?" Moral empathy, like physical empathy, is a feature of human "creatureliness," to use Karl Barth's term, and a creatureliness that guilt enables us to confront probably every single day.

I have often been with a person when death is coming in over the threshold. What is there then to say? We recite a final confessional: "Forgive me for all my sins which I have committed in my lifetime." When physical frailty is most overwhelming, so is moral frailty.

Gustave Flaubert's *Madame Bovary* tells the story of a woman who has led a dissolute life and comes, ultimately, to an unhappy end. As her last moments approach, a priest comes and gives her a crucifix. She glues her lips to it. Then the priest delivers the "sacrament of the anointing of the sick (extreme unction)," and he dips his right thumb in the oil beginning the unctions,

> . . . anointing her, first on the eyes which had gazed so covetously on the luxuries of the world; then, on the nostrils that had delighted in the breeze's soft caress and in all love-laden perfumes; then, on the mouth, the gateway of her lies, that had moaned in the moments of triumphant passion and cried aloud in the delirium of the senses; then, on the hands which had loved all things gentle to the touch; and, lastly, on the soles of the feet that, aforetime, had sped so swiftly to the appeasement of her desires, and now would stir no more.

Madame Bovary loses some of her terribly pallid color, "and her countenance . . . assumed an expression of serenity, as though the Sacrament had made her whole again."

Purity. Purity is not to be found in the desires of one's heart, as worthwhile as many of those desires may be. Purity is to be found in God. "I desire not the death of the sinner but that he should return and win new life" (Ezekiel 18:23). The search for purity is a lifelong search. Hopefully it comes. Even if with the last human breath.

To overcome our impurity, then, we must be led through a moral dimension, which we have carefully discussed. But beyond that, we need to reattach ourselves to our source. And that source, as we have now seen, is God.

WHERE IS GOD?

Do not be afraid of thinking about God. Do not be afraid of searching for God, even though such thoughts may seem inappropriate in a secular world. It is, I think, precisely in such a world that such thoughts are most often likely to arise.

Any discussion about God frightens so many modern people away. They are often generous, though, assuming that philosophers, priests, ministers, and rabbis know something about God. But my experience is that most people know a great deal. They are simply unwilling or unable to come out of the closet and to conceptualize their experiences with reference to the "G" word.

People learn to sense God at the moments of great mystery in their lives. Sometimes this happens most readily when they are close to a death, someone else's, even if not their own. For death is so shocking to face. It can turn even Madame Bovary around. It can turn anyone around.

But as much as I have found people to have an uncanny sense of God's closeness when death is at hand, they are able to sense His presence also at the other door. For as much as you hear about there being no atheists in foxholes, it is also true of hospital delivery rooms.

I remember the terrible problem that a well-known professor had. He was proud of many of his accomplishments and among these he counted his atheism—until one fateful night, when his first child was born. He was asked, "What was it like?" "Both wonderful and terrible, too," he replied. "For I saw life coming into the world, and that was a wonderful thing. But I nearly, then, came to believe in God."

As a professor, though, he was protected by his "nearly." Shall we call him a lucky man?

A newborn child is still so close to his source. Go to a hospital nursery and you will see people who have not yet sinned! It is an extraordinary sight. Purity marks the life force that powerfully flows through the veins of an infant, and it is extraordinary to behold. The souls of infants are newcomers to the world. So recently uprooted from their divine source, they have not yet had the chance to forget God.

Time and living will yet take care of that.

But for all of us, our souls are like chimney sweeps in their stay in this world. You can hardly recognize their purity; you can hardly recognize their presence, they get so soiled.

This ethical inquiry will be of value if it does two things. If it clarifies what guilt is, how it works, why we cannot be ethical without paying its price, then it will have accomplished one task. But since this inquiry is an inquiry into *theological* ethics, it will finally help on another level. It will help if it brings souls closer to God: not only to reroute the actions of those who are concerned to do right, but to reroot the person in the source of these actions—in God.

GOD REMEMBERS

One of the great advantages of sensing the reality of God is in the fringe benefits that come along with it. Simply knowing God is there gives believers less cause for anxiety in certain areas of their lives. And one part of that reality is particularly helpful in making it possible to overcome some of the lasting uneasiness that comes from our guilt.

It is the certainty that God remembers. To most people, this is a problem with God. When talking about guilt, indeed, this might seem to be a problem. Wouldn't it be more pleasant to believe that God forgets? Then we would have no accounting to worry about in the future!

But think of the plus: if He remembers, then you have a chance to forget. For example, those imperfect creatures—your friends and enemies who have wronged you and who have filled you with enough anger to last forever, that no-good someone whom you have every right to detest until his dying day—you can forget them.

Forget? And let them get away with it? But haven't I argued throughout this book for the importance of accountability?

I certainly have. But God will remember. You can take advantage of God's concern to take a load off your own mind, and to forget.

If God remembers, then we can afford to forget the pains and disappointments of our lives. How many of us will continue to carry around with us the pain of not having achieved our goals?

Some businessmen always see the worst year in front of them at night. This makes for cautious planning indeed, but it also makes for endless sleepless nights, something we could do well to live without. The disappointments of the marketplace are registered not only in dollars and cents, but sometimes in heartache and the sense of all-encompassing failure which they bring.

But if these disappointments are eating at you deeply, you ought to remember that you have a chance to forget. God will remember your travail, and you are free to be renewed.

If God remembers, I am sure it means that He keeps good notes as He hears the arguments we have as husbands and wives. God knows when one of us is right and when the other one is right, too.

But with us, anger can turn to enmity. That resentment can grow, and, like the radiation leaking from a disabled reactor, these hidden forces will slowly work on a person's constitution until they destroy him in toto.

If God remembers, then He remembers the reasons for our resentments, and He knows who is right. But God has so much love and mercy that He can tolerate all those problems better than you or I. What should we do? We should forget our anger so that we can find our loved ones again.

There are two kinds of anger which many of us feel, and which are healthy to forget: anger at God and anger at ourselves.

People suffer from sickness, bereavement, setbacks, at many times in life. They express their anger to God. And this is good. Why not tell Him what we think? Why has He caused so much suffering? Those who have suffered terribly may sometimes have a good claim against God.

Be careful, here. For you must remember that your claim may not be so good. It may simply be an excuse that shows a weakness in your faith.

On the other hand, if your claim is good, I recommend that you put it in God's hands. The greatest mysteries of suffering are beyond the understanding of us all. Let God worry about the inconsistencies in His universe that bother us. If we can do this, there is an obvious practical advantage. We can forget. We can forget the anger we feel at God, and if we do that we will remove a great burden from our backs.

But the most difficult anger of all is the anger we feel at ourselves. At the root of so much hatred is a tarnished self-image. Central to our concern in this book has been the effort to enable us to live pleasantly and fulfillingly with ourselves, even though we are so much less than we ought to be.

Remember, though, that there is only One who keeps a full ledger on our lives, in which our signatures are found. But that One is filled with more love and mercy than you will find in any human being. God remembers. Let us therefore forget the imperfections which are so palpable when we think about ourselves.

FROM ANGER TO LOVE

Do you know why it is such a great boon, this gift to be able to forget the anger and resentments which have piled up in our lives? Because the hatreds that occupy our thoughts and our feelings draw away the energy of our emotions from more important concerns.

In *The Scarlet Letter*, Nathaniel Hawthorne describes human beings filled with anger and hate. When one of them, the man known as Roger Chillingworth, finds that the object of his hate has died, he loses the emotional force of his life.

But at that point, Hawthorne muses on the great power of hatred and on its bedfellow: love. They are so much alike. "Each," Hawthorne says, "in its utmost development, supposes a high degree of intimacy. . . . Each renders one individual dependent for the food of his affections and spiritual life upon another."

Hawthorne's insight about the intimate connection between the emotions of hate and love is the point around which so much turns in spiritual life. Why, after all, unburden ourselves, why unburden our hearts of the enmities we feel toward God, toward ourselves, toward ever so many other human beings? Why try to overcome guilt, why try to rise beyond its message of the need to be better?

Why? So that we can love. So that we can be unburdened to the degree that we can fully love. That we can fully love ourselves, that we can fully love other human beings. That we can fully love God.

The message of this long tale of liberation is simple in essence. It is a tale designed to release the feelings that cannot be properly released. It is a prescription to allow for loving more, and better, and of being able to love and be good at the same time.

The purpose of focusing on guilt is not, ultimately, to make us feel bad for our wrongdoings. It is to free us from the constraints that have made it difficult, if not impossible, to love as we know we can.

To do that, we should not be afraid of our feelings, even our feelings of guilt. Feeling guilty is the beginning, not the end. To do that, we should not let ourselves think that the question: "Do you have a guilty conscience?" can only be accompanied by a sardonic grin. Rather, a guilty conscience brings each of us in contact with our own rational powers, with our own moral freedom, and with the power that being ethical places in each of our hands.

We need not to be debilitated by guilt, but to fight back, to channel guilt properly into creative actions, into liberating feelings. And while that process is a process that takes a lifelong time to complete, it is one that reaps benefit for other people, for our society and its moral burdens, and for ourselves. It is a process that brings us back to God.

God enables us wandering, rootless creatures to attach ourselves to Him. That having begun, God allows us to unburden our hearts and thereby to become pure. As the Scriptures say: "Before the Lord you become pure" (Leviticus 16:30). And, finally, that rooted plant can flower. That purified human being can turn to every other person motivated by one emotion and one alone—by love.

And that is why Rabbi Akiba says: "Happy are you O Israel; Who purifies you? If not your Father who is in Heaven?"[3]

How happy are we when we are finally freed to love!

Notes

CHAPTER 1

[1] See the remark of James Strachey, who translated and edited from the German Sigmund Freud's *Civilization and Its Discontents* (New York: W. W. Norton and Co., Inc., 1962), p. 82, n.1.

[2] *The New York Times Magazine*, March 9, 1986, p. 73.

CHAPTER 2

[1] Laurel Richardson, *The New Other Woman: Contemporary Single Women in Affairs with Married Men* (New York: The Free Press, 1985), pp. 88–92.

[2] *Vogue*, July 1986, p. 20.

[3] Gerald G. Jampolsky, M.D., with Patricia Hopkins and William N. Thetford, Ph.D., *Good-Bye to Guilt: Releasing Fear Through Forgiveness* (New York: Bantam, 1985), p. 33.

[4] Ibid., p. 212.

[5] *Newsday Magazine*, June 30, 1985.

[6] Barbara Grizzuti Harrison, "How to Find Time to Do Nothing," *Self*, July 1985.

[7] Muriel R. Gillick, "Health Promotion, Jogging, and the Pursuit of the Moral Life," *Journal of Health Politics, Policy and Law*, Vol. 9, No. 3, Fall 1984.

[8] Glenn Collins, *How to Be a Guilty Parent* (New York: Times Books, 1983).

[9] *The New York Times*, December 5, 1985.

[10] Reinhold Niebuhr, *An Interpretation of Christian Ethics* (New York: Harper & Row, 1963), p. 147.

CHAPTER 3

[1] *The New Yorker*, August 19, 1985.

[2] Gabrielle Taylor, *Pride, Shame and Guilt: Emotions of Self-Assessment* (Oxford, England: Clarendon Press, 1985).

[3] Willard Gaylin, *Feelings: Our Vital Signs* (New York: Harper & Row, 1979).

[4] William Shakespeare, *Macbeth*, Act II, ii.

[5] Maimonides, *The Eight Chapters*, Ch. 3.

[6] Pinhas Peli, *On Repentance: In the Thought and Oral Discourses of Rabbi Joseph B. Soloveitchik* (Jerusalem: Orot, 1980), p. 212.

CHAPTER 4

[1] James Joyce, *A Portrait of the Artist as a Young Man* (Norwalk, Conn.: Easton, 1977), p. 134.

[2] Karl Menninger, M.D., *Whatever Became of Sin?* (New York: Hawthorn, 1973), p. 2.

[3] Walter Kiechel, III, "The Guilt-edged Executive," *Fortune*, May 28, 1984.

[4] *The Ways of the Righteous*, author unknown, Ch. 3. See also Abraham Joshua Heschel, *The Insecurity of Freedom* (New York: Schocken, 1972), pp. 124–125.

[5] B. Jacob, *The First Book of the Bible: GENESIS*, abridged, ed. and trans. by Ernest I. Jacob and Walter Jacob (New York: KTAV, 1974), pp. 31–32.

CHAPTER 5

[1] *People*, November 26, 1984, p. 99.

[2] Ibid.

[3] Garth Wood, *The Myth of Neurosis: Overcoming the Illness Excuse* (New York: Harper & Row, 1986), p. 135.

[4] Ibid., p. 145.

[5] Ibid.

[6] Robert Coles, "Harvard Diary," *New Oxford Review,* Vol. 51, No. 6, September 1984, pp. 12–14. I am grateful to Rabbi Elie Spitz for having shown me this article.

[7] Ibid., p. 14.

CHAPTER 6

[1] See Harry A. Wolfson, *The Philosophy of the Kalam* (Cambridge: Harvard, 1976), Ch. 9.

[2] Maimonides, *The Eight Chapters,* Ch. 8.

[3] Ibid., Ch. 1.

CHAPTER 7

[1] Lynn Caine, *What Did I Do Wrong? Mothers, Children, Guilt* (New York: Arbor House, 1985).

[2] *People,* May 27, 1985, p. 112.

[3] Gloria Norris and Joann Miller, "Motherhood and Guilt," *Working Woman,* April 1984, p. 159.

[4] *The Reader's Digest,* August 1986.

[5] Russell Baker, "Intimations of Mortality," *The New York Times Magazine,* February 28, 1988.

[6] Paul Cowan, "In the Land of the Sick," *The Village Voice,* May 17, 1988.

CHAPTER 8

[1] *Working Woman,* April 1984. I hasten to add that their rule number two counsels: "Don't instantly jump to the conclusion that your working is the cause of every problem that occurs."

[2] *U.S. News and World Report,* April 30, 1984.

CHAPTER 9

[1] Ronald M. Green, *Religion and Moral Reason: A New Method for Comparative Study* (New York: Oxford University Press, 1988), p. 3.

CHAPTER 10

[1] See Rabbi Israel Alnakawa, *Sefer Menorat Hamaor*, Ch. 3.

[2] Rabbi Joseph B. Soloveitchik, "The Halakhah of the First Day," in Jack Riemer, ed., *Jewish Reflections on Death* (New York: Schocken, 1974), p. 81.

[3] Green, p. 3.

[4] Midrash Bereshit Rabbah 12:15.

CHAPTER 11

[1] Martin Hengel, *The Atonement: The Origins of the Doctrine in the New Testament* (Philadelphia: The Fortress Press, 1981), pp. 24–25.

[2] Yehezkel Kaufmann, *Toldot Ha-Emunah Ha-Yisraelit (The Religion of Israel)* (Jerusalem: Mosad Bialik, 1959), V (Vol. 2, Book 2), p. 408.

CHAPTER 12

[1] Bernard J. Verkamp, "Moral Treatment of Returning Warriors in the Early Middle Ages," *The Journal of Religious Ethics*, Vol. 16, No. 2, Fall 1988, p. 235.

[2] John Rawls, *A Theory of Justice* (Cambridge: Harvard, 1971), p. 444.

[3] Kenneth Clark, *The Nude: A Study in Ideal Form* (Garden City, N.Y.: Doubleday, 1956), p. 48.

[4] Ibid., p. 49.

[5] Aristotle, *Nichomachean Ethics* (VIII, 8, 1159b, 6–7).

[6] Note that the Hebrew word *tamim*, which can be translated as "blameless" or "perfect," appears in the Bible as a goal, most often as an exhortation to imitate God. See Genesis 17:1, where the Lord appears to Abraham and says: "Walk in my ways and be blameless." Similarly, Deuteronomy 18:13. When Noah is described as being *tamim*, the phrase is qualified by ". . . in his age." When David describes himself as *tamim* (2 Samuel 22:24), his words of hubris can only be excused by the context: the exultation of having triumphed in battle. David was far from perfect! Only God is perfect: "The Rock!—His deeds are perfect" (Deuteronomy 32:4).

[7] See Harry A. Wolfson, *Philo* (Cambridge: Harvard, 1968), Vol. II, p. 253.

[8] Note that our own modern preoccupation with guilt as a result of eating foods that are too caloric is, of course, a result of how *imperfect* our bodies are when compared to an ideal that we share. Once again, it is imperfection that leads to guilt.

[9] According to the rabbinic interpretation of Leviticus 4:13.

[10] Pinhas Peli, "Torah Today," in the *Jerusalem Post,* International Edition, week ending March 22, 1986.

[11] Midrash Tanhuma, Tazria.

CHAPTER 13

[1] Chronicles 20:1; 2 Samuel 11:1; 1 Kings 20:26.

[2] 1 Samuel 7:17. See Pinhas Peli, *Jerusalem Post*, International Edition, week ending September 17, 1988.

[3] Such as Hosea 7:10 and 14:2, or Nehemiah 1:9. Interestingly, it can also be used in the opposite way, meaning a return to un-Godly ways as in Joshua 22:16.

[4] See Max Scheler, "Repentance and Rebirth," in *On the Eternal in Man* (Hamden: Shoe String, 1972), pp. 33–65, and J. B. Soloveitchik, "The Voice of My Beloved Knocketh" (Hebrew), in *Divrei Hegut v'Ha'arakhah* (Jerusalem: World Zionist Organization, 5743), pp. 9–16.

[5] Adin Steinsaltz, *Teshuvah: A Guide for the Newly Observant Jew* (New York: The Free Press, 1987), p. 5.

[6] See the essay by Rabbi Joseph B. Soloveitchik entitled "Acquittal and Purification," in Pinhas H. Peli, *On Repentance in the Thought and Oral Discourses of Rabbi Joseph B. Soloveitchik* (Jerusalem: Orot, 1980), pp. 57–74, and particularly the analysis of Rabbi Soloveitchik's ideas found in the essay "Human Renewal—The Courage to Change" (Jerusalem: The Shalom Hartman Institute for Advanced Judaic Studies, 1983).

[7] See Scheler, pp. 36–37.

[8] Jerusalem Talmud Makkot 2:6 (2:7 in Krotoschin ed.); Pesikta d'Rav Kahana, ed. Solomon Buber, 158b.

[9] Talmud Yoma 85b.

[10] Talmud Pesahim 54a.

[11] See, for example, Maimonides, *Mishneh Torah*, "Laws of Repentance" 1:1; 2:1; Saadia Gaon, *Book of Beliefs and Opinions*, Ch. 7; Bahya ibn Paquda, *The Book of Direction to the Duties of the Heart*, Ch. 7; Jonah ben Abraham Gerondi, *The Gates of Repentance*.

CHAPTER 14

[1] This analysis follows the discussion by J. B. Soloveitchik in Peli's *On Repentance*, pp. 216–219.

[2] Ike Flores, The Associated Press, January 25, 1989.

[3] The Associated Press, February 23, 1989.

[4] *The New York Times*, March 13, 1986.

[5] Talmud Rosh Hashanah 16b.

[6] January 17, 1989.

[7] Maimonides, *Mishneh Torah*, "Laws of Repentance" 2:2.

[8] Steinsaltz, p. 6.

[9] The Associated Press, December 30, 1989.

[10] Psalms 32:1.

[11] Leviticus 5:15–16; 20–27.

[12] See Louis Ginzberg, "Rabbi Israel Salanter," in *The Jewish Expression*, ed. Judah Goldin (New Haven: Yale), pp. 427–438, and Hillel Goldberg, "Israel Salanter and '*Orhot Zaddikim:* Restructuring Musar Literature,' " *Tradition*, Vol. 23, No. 4, Summer 1988.

[13] *The New York Times*, March 21, 1988.

[14] Talmud Shabbat 153a.

CHAPTER 15

[1] *Zikhron la-Rishonim*, brought in S. Y. Agnon, *Days of Awe* (New York: Schocken, 1965), p. 26.

[2] Martin Buber, "The Way of Man, According to the Teachings of Hasidism," in *Hasidism and Modern Man*, ed. and trans. by Maurice Friedman (New York: Harper & Row, 1966).

[3] Mishnah Yoma 1:5.

[4] Milton Steinberg, "Our Persistent Failures," in *A Believing Jew* (New York: Harcourt, Brace and Co., 1951), pp. 213–228.

[5] Paul Tillich, "You Are Accepted," in *The Shaking of the Foundations* (New York: Charles Scribner's Sons, 1948), pp. 156–157.

[6] Pesach Krauss and Morrie Goldfischer, *Why Me? Coping with Grief, Loss, and Change* (New York: Bantam, 1988).

[7] Ibid., p. 33.

[8] Tillich, "You are Accepted," p. 162.

[9] In *Abraham Isaac Kook,* trans. and intro. by Ben Zion Bokser (New York, Paulist Press, 1978).

[10] Ibid., p. 104.

[11] Jane Vonnegut Yarmolinsky, *Angels Without Wings* (Boston: Houghton Mifflin, 1987), p. 174.

CHAPTER 16

[1] Erich Fromm, *The Art of Loving* (London: George Allen & Unwin, Ltd., 1957), p. 41.

[2] See "The Other Side of Selfish," by Kathleen Madden, *Vogue,* August 1988, p. 315.

[3] Buber, p. 252.

[4] Mishnah Yoma 8:9; Maimonides, *Mishneh Torah,* "Laws of Repentance" 2:9–11.

[5] Nan Robertson, *Getting Better: Inside Alcoholics Anonymous* (New York: William Morrow, 1988), p. 70.

[6] *The New York Times,* February 2, 1989.

[7] Ibid., October 4, 1986.

CHAPTER 17

[1] Edmund Burke, "Second Speech on Conciliation with America. The Thirteen Resolutions" (March 22, 1775).

[2] See, for example, 2 Kings 21:10–15, Joshua 7, and Isaiah 65:7.

[3] Mishnah Sotah 9:6.

[4] See, for example, the fascinating book *Born Guilty: Children of Nazi Families* (New York: Basic Books, 1988).

[5] Rabbi Abraham Isaac Hacohen Kook, *The Lights of Penitence*, in Ben Zion Bokser, trans. and ed., *Abraham Isaac Kook* (New York: Paulist Press, 1978), p. 56.

[6] Maimonides, *Mishneh Torah*, "Laws of Repentance" 3:8.

[7] Kook, ibid.

[8] *The New York Times*, October 25, 1985.

CHAPTER 18

[1] Mishnah Terumot 9:7.

[2] Elaine Pagels, *Adam, Eve, and the Serpent* (New York: Random House, 1988), pp. 127–150.

[3] Mishnah Yoma 8:9.

Index

About the Author

Dr. Harlan J. Wechsler is rabbi of Congregation Or Zarua in Manhattan, and Visiting Assistant Professor of Philosophy at The Jewish Theological Seminary of America, where he teaches theology and ethics. A graduate of Harvard College, with both ordination and a Ph.D. from The Jewish Theological Seminary, he is chairman of the board of the Hospital Chaplaincy in New York City.

Happiest when teaching an ancient text to young rabbis-to-be or to the many laymen who come to study with him, Rabbi Wechsler dreams of the spruce-covered mountains that come down to the sea by his Southwest Harbor, Maine, home. Much of this book was written there. And he believes that theology and religion can make the world a better and a more peaceful place.